Photography by Christian Sarramon

Paris Patisseries

History • Shops • Recipes

Foreword by Pierre Hermé

Flammarion

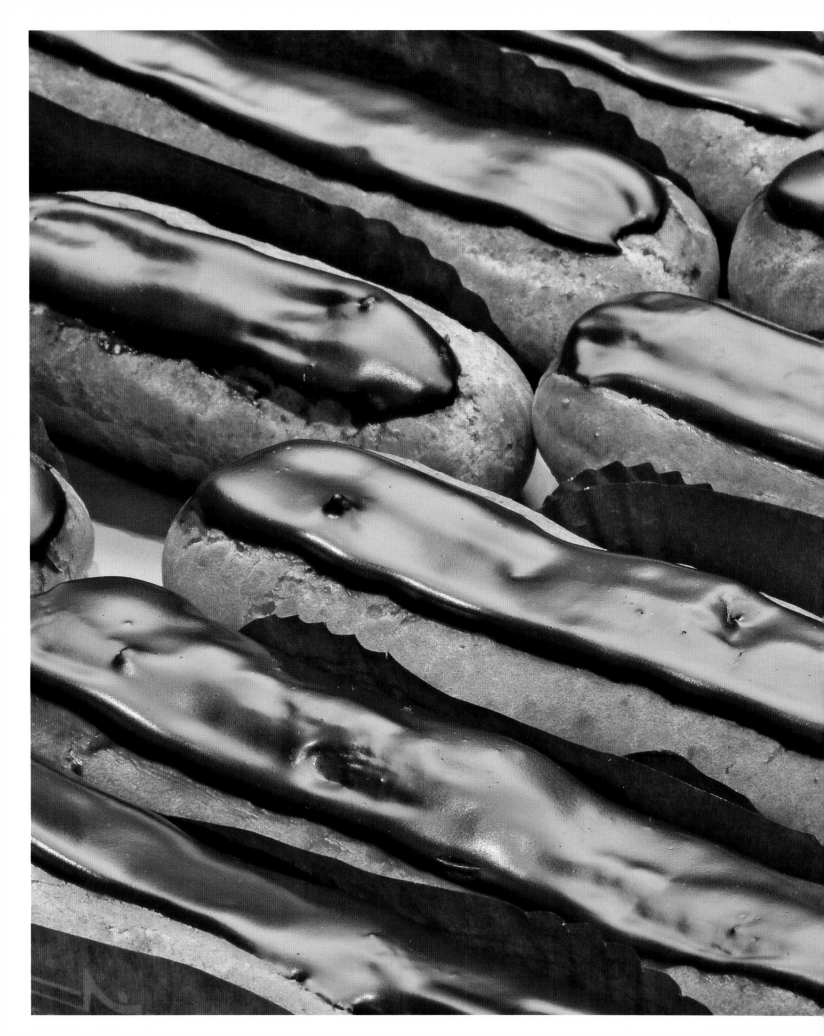

Contents

Nineteenth-century decoration in the Stohrer boutique: Allegory of Fame bearing a pyramid of *puits d'amour* (p. 1); strawberry Suprême by Laurent Duchêne (p. 2); éclairs at the Maison du Chocolat (p. 4–5). Above and facing page, from left to right, Pierre Hermé's renowned Ispahan macaroons, delicate tarts served at the *salon de thé* of ice-cream maker Berthillon, chocolate Feuille d'Automne from Lenôtre, variously flavored macaroons by Nathalie Robert and Didier Mathray, palmiers, and the shop front of the Maison Stohrer, a listed building.

P. 92
Contemporary Creations

Just like the fashion designers
for whom Paris is so renowned,
contemporary pastry chefs
create new gateaux each
season, showcasing surprising
combinations, new aesthetics, and
astonishing designs. Increasingly
lighter cakes containing exotic
ingredients are enhanced by the
flavor of caramel with fleur de sel,
ever more imaginative macaroons
are concocted, and miniature
desserts are served in shot glasses
to make *verrines*. Today's creations
are certain to become tomorrow's
classics.

P. 126
Viennoiseries
and Treats To Go

These are cakes to eat warm
from the baker's oven. Indulge
yourself with croissants, chocolate
rolls, brioches, and turnovers
at breakfast, or for an afternoon
snack on the go. At teatime,
serve loaf cakes, genoise
sponge, chocolate chip cookies,
and madeleines.

P. 161
Our Favorite Addresses
and Recipes for Parisian
Patisseries

Where can you find these delectable
treats? Who should be your trusted
purveyor of macaroons and brioche?
We will take you on a guided tour
of the best pastry shops of Paris, the
world's gourmand capital, and show
you the places where teatime has
been elevated to a high art form.

As a bonus, you will find
the recipes the best pastry chefs have
shared with us so that you
can prepare delicious treats to serve
at your own table.

Foreword

Pastries are a promise of sweetness, a tangible expression of a pastry maker's audacious dreams. Their tastes and fragrances evoke memories.

The creative dimension of pastry making means that it is an art form. It is a craft too, involving the daily making of cakes, tarts, macaroons, ice creams, candies, and other treats. In the kitchen of each of the pastry shops mentioned here, craftspeople who are passionate about their work devote themselves to transforming prime ingredients into sublime creations.

Paris Patisseries gives a complete overview of the pastries of Paris: from the traditional rum babas, madeleines, éclairs, and mille-feuilles to the creative innovations that will certainly become classics. There is a special place for chocolate and for the oh-so-Parisian *viennoiseries*.

This book lists all the best pastry shops, from the most famous and well established to those that have come into being over the past two decades, and includes some of their recipes. Let yourself be guided through Paris to discover its best, most delectable treats.

Pierre Hermé

The stories conveyed by desserts are stories

of nostalgic affection that become part of family lore. They accompany landmarks in our lives, bringing a touch of tenderness and sweetness to all generations of sweet lovers. The classic desserts of the French pastry tradition have come down to us through time, thanks to the specialties of each master pastry maker, some of whom have created such outstanding desserts that their recipes go back several centuries. They are often desserts that the French know from childhood, when they were the highlight of Sunday lunches, birthday parties, and celebrations. They bring back fond memories; as Parisians grow into adults, they seek out their flavors, textures, and scents. Parisians are always ready to cross the city from one end to the other to fetch *the* cake whose mere mention makes their mouths water.

Cakes are often enjoyed with family and friends; they can also provide a special, private treat, one that could be termed purely selfish. Small cakes can make good companions, provide consolation, and soothe our nerves. They may reward us for an accomplishment or mark an occasion we are alone to celebrate. For some, they are a ritual, a regular part of the day. Cakes are even known to have powers of seduction, calling on our gourmand instincts and whims. Take a walk along the streets of Paris—the pastry shop windows are always so tempting it is hard not to enter; point at just the cake that has caught your fancy, and utter the words, "That one, please."

We all have our favorites, the cakes we go back to, but in these pastry shops you may well find a cake that will surprise you, intrigue you, or give your senses a wake-up call. You may find it amusing, luscious, outlandish, or it may just appeal to the gourmand in you. And that is what cakes are meant to do: be attractive, amaze you, and simply be irresistible, the better to be eaten.

Whatever our preference—tarts, madeleines, mille-feuilles, éclairs, Saint Honorés, rum babas—the best versions of the different patisseries will never fail to delight. And in this book we only show the best, the truly exceptional. Some cakes have come down through the centuries; some have suffered at the hands of unworthy pastry makers or even gone out of fashion. Since the late 1970s, they have undergone a revival, thanks to Gaston Lenôtre, who revisited the French pastry-making heritage. He rid cakes of their embellishments made of spun sugar and marzipan, and lightened up their cream, butter, and sugar content. The wonderful creations of Nicolas Stohrer, Vincent de la Chapelle, Antonin Carême, the Jullien brothers, Chiboust, and other illustrious pastry chefs have taken on new life. These lighter versions mean we can digest them easily and with only a hint of guilt. Pierre Hermé, a worthy student of Lenôtre, has surpassed his master by bringing us ever more airy, subtle, and unexpected creations.

All these timely changes mean that some desserts no longer look or taste quite like the originals, or those we used to love. Today, a breath of modernity is blowing over time-honored desserts and giving them a new dimension.

Rose, raspberry, and litchi combine to create the subtle harmonies of Pierre Hermé's Ispahan (p. 8). Lemon, strawberry, and matcha tea creations from Sadaharu Aoki (pp. 10–11). Raspberry-flavored hearts at Pain de Sucre, a perfect Valentine's Day treat (facing page).

Cakes from our Childhood

Tarts, *Religieuses*, and Meringues

DES GÂTEAUX ET DU PAIN
The classic Gâteau Saint Honoré, revisited by Claire Damon with contemporary flavors. Under its white icing, the choux pastry is filled with a milk chocolate cream, and the chantilly cream is flavored with orange-blossom water (page 15).

ALAIN PASSARD
A Bouquet of Roses, this stunning apple tart (facing page) was created by this great chef for his restaurant, L'Arpège. A delectable three-star dessert, it is the culmination of an elegant dinner.

1 Today the French term "*macaron*" is occasionally used even by English speakers to differentiate the French double-decker almond macaroon from other versions of this pastry, e.g., the American coconut macaroon. It should be noted that the macaroons in this book are all almond macaroons (see page 101).

Ask anyone who grew up in Paris and they will fondly remember the special happiness of ogling the cream cake creations in the window of a pastry shop, cakes they have known since they were very young. A particular pleasure for gourmands is the sight of mille-feuilles, rum babas, éclairs, choux pastry, towering Saint Honorés, tarts, and other traditional cakes from the French pastry repertoire. A mere glimpse of them sends the food-lover directly into the pastry shop with an irrepressible urge to taste these sweet flavors and crisp, creamy, or crunchy textures. But this urge runs into an obstacle: the profusion of choice. It is impossible to taste the entire array—or at least, not all at the same time. Each pastry gives off smooth, heady smells. Each entices the eye with its colors—glossy, vivid, or gentle. Each speaks of sweetness and voluptuousness. For some, they are memories of rewards, comfort, and even consolation. These works of art encased in puff pastry, choux pastry, sweet crusts, and sponge cake are desirable rarities that most home bakers would not dare to attempt. The unseen complexity that contributes to their perfection results from the skills of a professional pastry chef who works with scientific precision to first provide a feast for our eyes before their subtle compositions are revealed to our palates.

To think that for centuries there were no desserts—or at least not as we know them today. For many years, desserts comprised an extended range of fruit, many of which are no longer cultivated, and which were eaten raw, candied (comfit), in marmalades, and in compotes. They were accompanied by dry biscuits, and were also often eaten as snacks. From the early Middle Ages onward, *pasticiers-hashiers* (from the Old French verb *pasticier*, "to make pastry"), as they were known, prepared "huff pastes" to seal meat and fish during cooking. This "*pasté*" was usually savory, but it was also found in a sweet version with fruit (pear pasties). Do bear in mind that most of the pastries we eat today, like tarts, pies, fritters, and creams were not served at the end of the meal but as sweet *entremets*— literally, between other courses. Meringues, almond macaroons or *macarons* as they are known in France[1], and gingerbread were also baked.

PAIN DE SUCRE

Pain de Sucre's Baobob is a
reinterpretation of a great
classic, the rum baba. The
pipette contains rum-vanilla
punch, allowing you to soak
your cake as you wish
(page 18). Beneath the
original colored-glass ceiling,
the long, very contemporary
counter showcases a
ravishing display of
multicolored cakes and
pastries (page 19).

BISTROT PAUL BERT

In this traditional Parisian
bistro (above right), here are
the desserts not to be missed:
the savarin with its whipped
cream center (above left) and
the Paris-Brest, with its
unctuous praline cream in a
crisp choux pastry (facing
page). It's a cake that's too
delicate to serve in summer.

In the eighteenth century, the foundations of modern pastry making were laid and innovative techniques developed. In France, Vincent de La Chapelle wrote his treatise, *Le Cuisinier Modern* (The Modern Cook); in 1746 *La Cuisinière Bourgeoise* (The Bourgeois Cook) was published with great success, contributing to the spread of a considerable number of pastry recipes hitherto known only in the courts of nobles. But it was only in the nineteenth century that the cake as we know it was born. Pastry chefs let their imaginations run wild; they set themselves increasing challenges to astonish the bourgeois class that now reigned supreme in the Industrial Age. The bourgeois in France imitated the aristocrats who had suffered during the French Revolution. They organized splendid parties, large banquets, and interminable family meals, culminating in a dessert that had to be as dazzling as the pompous procession of rich dishes that led up to it. A grand Saint Honoré, with its tower of cream puffs filled with pastry cream, its crème Chiboust, all drizzled with caramel, or a *croquembouche* (literally, "crunch in the mouth"), a conical pile of small choux pastries on a nougat base, would make an eye-catching, spectacular entrance and, when served, would be certain to please the palate. This is how the sophisticated sweets created by pastry chefs who officiated in Paris such as Nicolas Stohrer, Vincent de la Chapelle, Antonin Carême, the Jullien brothers, and Chiboust came to be—and have remained—the stars of the storefront windows of pastry shops. In the 1930s, Ladurée developed an innovative concept, a *salon de thé*, a cross between a Parisian café and a pastry shop. After the Second World War, such *salons* spread and, with them, the trend of producing individual cakes.

Toward the end of the 1970s, pastry making underwent a rejuvenation. One man was largely responsible for this, and homage should be paid to Gaston Lenôtre, the true inventor of modern pastry. He revisited traditional French pastry making, ridding it of its superfluous decorations and reducing the cream, butter, and sugar content. Moving away from old-fashioned practices, he reinterpreted the

great classics. "Thanks to him, a new generation, with Pierre Hermé at its helm, established themselves and brought triumph to one of the world's most famous pastry schools," wrote François Simon, the gastronomic critic of the French daily *Le Figaro*, in tribute to the master pastry chef.

From tarts to rum babas, from mille-feuilles to Paris-Brest (a bicycle-wheel-shaped choux pastry filled with hazelnut cream), the repertoire of cakes available to us today was born of an exact science: pastry making. This science is constantly seeking to combine textures to create a balance and harmony of flavors, to please the eye as much as the palate. Many great pastry chefs have labored to transmit the skills and knowledge that they have used to complement their genius.

For many people, the first pastry-linked emotion goes back to when they were very young. In France, the desserts that children were allowed to eat were the flan, a custard tart; the clafoutis, a flan with cherries; and fruit tarts. The slice of custard tart would be bought at the bakery closest to school, and made for a delightful afternoon snack that added cheer to the walk home. Its crust had to be either pie- or shortcrust, or very thin, and the custard texture soft and a little wobbly, thanks to a perfect balance between the flour or cornstarch with the eggs and milk.

The tart is the perfect dessert for a family meal. We can probably all remember our mothers and grandmothers creating fruit tarts for us as children; we would watch closely as they prepared them step by step. To this day, memories surface of the heady fragrances of sugar, fruit, and crust as they mingled during baking. When we consider the history of cakes, we see that the tart is the dessert that has come down to us through the ages, keeping the simplicity of a Middle Age dish. It came into being when a baker had a stroke of genius: to mix a little butter into his bread dough. The base has remained unchanged: pie- or shortcrust pastry, sweet pastry, or puff pastry topped with seasonal fruits. Tarts may be rustic looking, with a thick base and coarsely chopped apples that give a genuine fruity taste. They may be more refined and elegant if the apples are thinly sliced so that they soften and, when the tart is baked, the sugar from the fruits forms a thin layer of flavored caramel. It seems that the recipe for apple tart remained unchanged until the appearance of what is known as the tarte Tatin, the upside-down apple cake. The story of how this cake came into being is charming. In a small town in central France, Lamotte-Beuvron, two sisters ran an inn. One day, goes the legend, Stéphanie, the elder sister, placed her tart in the oven the wrong way round. It was during the hunting season, and the hungry hunters were due to arrive any minute. There was no time to make a new tart, so she

STOHRER
The *puits d'amour*, the "well of love": a traditional dessert that few pastry chefs make (pages 22–23). The vanilla cream is caramelized using a special iron.

PIERRE HERMÉ
Hermé's Surprise looks like a giant candy. The most melting meringue encases a mousseline cream whose flavor changes with the seasons (facing page).

DES GÂTEAUX ET DU PAIN
Claire Damon created this pistachio-strawberry cake for Mother's Day (below). The tangy notes of the strawberry compote add interesting nuances to the velvety pistachio cream.

sprinkled the mold with sugar, arranged the apple quarters at the bottom with a few knobs of butter, and covered it all with pieces of pastry so that the base would look presentable. The apples stewed gently under the crust, becoming tender, almost melting. The tart was eventually introduced to Parisian diners between the two world wars. It is important to choose the right variety of apple for this dessert, because not all types soften without breaking up. The tarte Tatin, now a classic of the French pastry repertoire, has kept its mystery: no one knows exactly what the caramel topping will be like when the cake is turned out of its mold—will it be too dark, not golden enough, or just right?

Another unusual tart is the lemon tart, for it does not contain a single piece of fruit. In 1651, François Massaliot wrote *Cuisinier François* (French Cook) in which he gave the recipe for a lemon tart called "admirable pie." The sour lemon cream is balanced by the lightly browned meringue that tops it. Recently, some of the better-known pastry chefs have begun using Massaliot's suggestion of incorporating candied zest mixed into the cream. With this method, they have replaced the meringue by a lemon jelly that not only gives a wonderful mirror effect but also results in an increased range of nuances of the citrus flavors.

Today, the fruit tarts made by pastry chefs are no longer simple or rustic, but sophisticated. They are strikingly beautiful, sometimes even taking on the appearance of flowerbeds that are so artfully arranged one is reluctant to demolish them.

But the creamy cakes that brought magic to the childhoods of so many have been lightened by today's skilled pastry chefs. Pastry cream and chantilly result from the virtual alchemy used to bring together ingredients to create the perfect texture, be it velvety, foamy, or even ethereal.

Creams like this are sheer bliss when used to fill delicate choux pastry cases. Everyone in France remembers eating this treat at a christening, a communion, or a wedding, when the *croquembouche*,

GÉRARD MULOT
In the kingdom of meringues, harmony reigns between the meringue with a ribbon of lightly caramelized sugar and the chantilly cream (page 26); this dessert should be eaten within two hours of purchase. In contrast, however, the traditional lemon tart (page 27) should survive a short trip from the boutique.

LA GRANDE EPICERIE DU BON MARCHÉ
A vertical mille-feuilles, with the puff pastry and vanilla cream as light as one could possibly want (facing page).

LES DEUX ABEILLES
This romantic *salon de thé* (above center) has one of the most tempting dessert trolleys imaginable. The tarte Tatin (above left) is divine, but the astonishingly light lemon tart, beneath its dome of meringue (above right), simply has to be tasted.

LENÔTRE

The Eléonore tart, named by
Gaston Lenôtre in honor of his
mother, is a traditional apple
tart from his native
Normandy. Here, chunky
apple pieces sit on a bed of
applesauce. The base is a
thin layer of puff pastry. Serve
this tart with a jar of well-
chilled, thick crème fraîche.

FAUCHON

The pink and silver decor of Fauchon's *salon de thé* and the design of the presentation counters (above) make the perfect showcase for the inventive, playful creations of Christophe Adam. Renowned for its almost infinite range of éclairs, the *salon* here revisits the traditional raspberry charlotte (facing page).

CARETTE

This patisserie of yesteryear has been successfully transformed. Hubert de Givenchy, nephew of the designer, has created a refined, elegant setting (page 34). In this shop with its *salon de thé*, small lamps throw a gentle light on the great classics: raspberry delights, giant chocolate macaroons, and Madagascar vanilla Saint Honoré (page 33).

a pyramid of choux pastry barely held together by a thin covering of caramelized syrup, was brought out. The children had to wait while the adults enthused over how high it was. Photos had to be taken. Then, and only then, were they allowed to eat their share of this culinary balancing act. It was the opportunity to experience the ineffable sensuality of pastry cream, an intimation of voluptuousness.

Choux pastry was invented by Popelini, pastry chef to Catherine de Médicis in the sixteenth century. This combination of butter, eggs, and flour is unique in that it is baked twice, first in a pot and then in the oven, where it swells like a soap bubble until it becomes a light, crisp, yet tender casing.

Choux pastry has given rise to any number of desserts in French pastry making. A national signature dessert is the éclair; these were created in the city of Lyon, around 1850. They are immediately recognizable by their long, thin shape and fondant glazing, the same flavor as the pastry cream with which it is filled. For some time, éclairs were either chocolate or coffee flavored. They are always individual cakes and are meant to be eaten in a few mouthfuls, hence their name, which means "lightning." Today, the pastry cream is sometimes replaced by one using mascarpone, lighter and smoother, as a base. This is what Pierre Hermé uses for his vanilla éclairs. Equally tempting are the bright colors of creams flavored with pistachio, pineapple, and raspberry. Fruits have conquered the hitherto very closed world of éclairs, but no one is complaining.

Another major classic of French pastry that goes back to the mid-nineteenth century is the *religieuse*, "the nun," comprising two round choux pastry cases, a smaller one topping a larger one. A delicate butter-cream trimming is reminiscent of a nun's wimple, and a little touch of the same butter cream on top adds the finishing touch to the nun's habit. It is said that this cake was created by the pastry chef, Frascati, in 1856 in Paris. It did not look exactly as it does now, but more closely resembled a nun. It was made of a round base of sweet crust on which were placed chocolate or coffee éclairs. The colors were those of the homespun cowl, and *voilà*, you had the nun's habit. The bodice was made of a perfectly shaped oval choux pastry, and the head was made of what we now call the "*religieuse*." The entire pastry was nearly 8 inches (20 centimeters) high. This impressive, high-standing creation had a wide collar and a *coif* or headpiece of butter cream. Today, only the Stohrer pastry shop makes this old-fashioned *religieuse* to order.

And now the Saint Honoré. It used to be the gâteau par excellence for festivities and important occasions, but fell out of fashion for several decades. Just a few years ago, it made an appearance

again. As chubby-cheeked as a little angel, as light as a cloud, it is both aesthetically pleasing and luscious. The traditional Saint Honoré, made according to the recipe of its creator, the pastry chef Chiboust, is a crown of caramel-syrup-coated choux pastries, in the center of which is a goodly serving of Chiboust cream, a vanilla-flavored pastry cream to which egg whites beaten with sugar are added while it is still hot. Renowned pastry chefs have concocted several variations on this theme, changing both the shape and the flavor. Pastry cream is replaced with a velvety cream to which pieces of fruit bring a tangy note. Today there are creams with passion fruit and mango, or strawberry, blackberry, and violet, and the colors are no longer pale but bright—yellow or mauve, depending on the season.

Choux pastry has provided endless inspiration for pastry chefs. The last creation dates back to 1891, the year when a bicycle race was inaugurated: the Paris-Brest circuit. A baker, whose shop was located in a neighborhood of Paris near the start of the race, decided to make a cake in honor of the occasion. He made a choux pastry in the shape of a bicycle wheel, cut it in two and filled it with hazelnut-flavored butter cream. He sprinkled it with roasted, slivered almonds and confectioners' sugar. The race was last run in 1951, but the cake continues to be made according to its traditional recipe. It is quite delicious and extraordinarily delicate.

Cream goes well with other types of pastry too. Puff pastry layered with cream offers food lovers another duo of textures. The mille-feuille, (literally, one thousand leaves), was invented in 1806 by a pastry chef who worked on the Rue du Bac in central Paris. He folded his puff pastry over a few extra times, giving it six turns altogether, to increase the "puffing" effect. Once the rectangles of pastry are baked, they are layered on top of each other, with a generous filling of vanilla-flavored pastry cream in between. The top layer of pastry is signed off, as it were, with a sprinkling of confectioners' sugar or a topping of white fondant icing. In actual fact, a mille-feuille contains 729 thicknesses of pastry. The mille-feuille was such an immediate, resounding success that the illustrious Académie Française, guardians of the French language, immediately allowed the word to go into the dictionary. And the mille-feuille is still a highly popular dessert, with its three rectangles of crisp, golden pastry—so delicate that it breaks as soon as it comes into contact with the teeth. Today's version is often lighter and fluffier, without losing any of its flavor. Although a modest cake, the mille-feuille elicits all sorts of emotional reactions—provided it is fresh. It is a cake that has to be eaten as soon as possible, since the passing of time detracts from its main attraction: the crispiness of the puff pastry.

PAIN DE SUCRE
An almond shortcrust, almond cream, and raspberries dotted with emerald green chopped pistachios: the raspberry Pirouette tart (facing page).

GÉRARD MULOT
You'll find classic tarts that are as good as they have always been, thanks to their soft textures and the fact that they highlight the fruit: here, pear-almond and apricot (below).

SÉBASTIEN DÉGARDIN
Dégardin is a young pastry chef who reinvents the great classics—an example is his hazelnut éclair—and makes perfect traditional cakes, like the *fraisier* (page 38) and, far more uncommon, the *polonaise* with its meringue dome (page 39).

BLÉ SUCRÉ

Near the Marché d'Aligre in the twelfth arrondissement, stop for a delectable treat at Fabrice Bourlat's boutique, one of the city's best (above left). His tarts are marvelous, as is everything else. Here are the classic pear tart (above right) and his original take on a tarte Tatin (facing page).

PLAZA ATHÉNÉE

In the calm, elegant hotel on Avenue Montaigne (following pages, left), the Galérie des Gobelins welcomes guests who come to enjoy Christophe Michalak's pastries. In 2005, he was named "Best Pastry Chef in the World." He enjoys using traditional recipes as a starting point for innovations. With this éclair, made with pure arabica coffee and 70 percent cacao bittersweet chocolate, he puts the pastry back on the upper echelons of stylishness (page 43).

Any mille-feuille worthy of the name cannot spend more than four hours in a pastry shop window. And so to buy any for a weekend treat, you will have to get up early, as by noon this demanding and somewhat capricious cake will have disappeared from quality pastry shops.

Another miraculous creation bringing together puff pastry and pastry cream is the *puits d'amour*—"well of love." Its dome of vanilla-flavored pastry cream is caramelized on top using a hot iron. This creates a beautiful, gleaming, bronze-like mirror, as fragile as crystal. The cake takes its name from a famous late nineteenth-century operetta, and has become hard to find in Paris. One establishment where it can still be bought is the attractive blue pastry shop of Stohrer, located on the Rue Montorgeuil in central Paris. They still use the original cake molds and the nineteenth-century recipe.

The founder of this illustrious pastry shop, Nicolas Stohrer, pastry maker to Stanislas Leczinski, the deposed king of Poland who was welcomed to France by Louis XV, created another wonderful cake for his patron: the *baba au rhum*, or rum baba. Stanislas was a real gourmand, and one day, while eating his kugelhopf, decided it was too dry and asked for some Malaga wine to be brought. In his native Poland, it was customary to drench a similar cake in wine from Hungary. The combination of the kugelhopf and Malaga wine was not entirely to his satisfaction, and the king suggested adding saffron to the wine. The next day, the pastry chef perfected the recipe and presented Stanislas with the cake. The king thoroughly enjoyed this new creation and named it the Ali Baba in honor of the hero of *The Thousand and One Nights*, a book he loved. Today, the Ali Baba's baby brother is available; it is in the shape of a cork and is called a baba.

The name was shortened in the twentieth century and has many aficionados, all with exacting demands as regards the quality of both the pastry and the rum. A good rum baba must have just the

right degree of sponginess. Some like it to be thoroughly soaked; others prefer it a little drier. It is said to be a man's dessert, and it seems that many men have a weakness for the rum baba.

Plagiarism is found in pastry making as in other occupations, and some plagiarized pastries have been truly successful. In 1845, Auguste Jullien, one of the Jullien brothers, used the same pastry as that used for the baba, and saturated it with old rum as soon as it came out of the oven, garnishing it with candied orange peel. A custom-made mold in the shape of a pretty coiled crown means the center of the cake can be filled with pastry cream, whipped cream, or fresh fruit. It takes its name from Jean-Anthelme Brillat-Savarin, the author of *La Physiologie du gout* (The Physiology of Taste) to whom the Jullien brothers wished to render ardent homage. Whether it's known as a rum baba or a savarin, it is best eaten without restraint!

Crème chantilly is another cream that is enjoyed without restraint, one to which everyone is partial—a wonderful invention. Many of its fans believe a good chantilly cream is the discreet yet unmistakable sign of a fine pastry chef or a good *salon de thé*.

Traditionally, crème chantilly was often served at the center of a large meringue case for Sunday dessert. Today, some pastry chefs still make this delicate, delicious cake comprising two meringue cases put together with chantilly cream and topped with a dome of more chantilly. Queen Marie Leczinska brought it to the French royal court and made it fashionable. Meringue actually came into being in 1720 in Merhinghen in the Duchy of Saxe-Coburg in Austria. A Swiss pastry chef by the name of Casparini thought that he would use up the egg whites that were not needed in his cakes. He whipped them together with powdered sugar and baked the resulting foamy mixture at a low heat to retain its airy lightness. The sweet crossed through Germany and the first meringues arrived in France via the city of Nancy at the court of King Stanislas, the incorrigible gourmand. The Académie Française

LADURÉE

For a dream wedding cake, you can depend on a venerable institution like Ladurée, who make pyramid-shaped displays out of macaroons or small choux pastries, and tiered chocolate *entremets* beautifully covered with a delicate layer of pistachio marzipan (facing page). The displays in Ladurée's shop windows (above center) resemble the sets of a baroque opera where the characters are the dreamy cakes, like the vanilla, rose, and raspberry Saint Honorés (above left and right). The ubiquitous macaroon: exotically flavored for a contemporary take, or pistachio flavored in traditional style (page 46). The *réligieuses* are made with rose petals and violet (page 47).

JEAN-PAUL HÉVIN
At this renowned chocolate maker's boutique (above left), not all the cakes are of chocolate. Here is Hévin's version of the meringue (above right). The Princesse is made with matcha tea; and meringue also nestles beneath vermicelli of puréed chestnut in his interpretation of the classic Mont Blanc (facing page).

ANGELINA
A hot chocolate in this elegant *salon de thé* will be an unforgettable experience (page 50). But it's hard to resist the delicious Mont Blanc, its signature dessert (page 51). Eat it at any time of the day, or order a large one for a sumptuous ending to a celebratory meal. People come here from far and wide to collect their orders for Christmas dinner.

waited until 1804 (by which time the Revolution—during which no indulgence towards sweets was shown—had passed) to change the spelling of the dessert by removing the all-too Germanic "h"s in the original name to give "*meringue*."

Meringues are also a perfect accompaniment for chestnut cream; in fact, each enhances the other. Under the name of Mont Blanc, reminiscent of the high, perpetually snow-capped mountain, the two are combined: a meringue case encloses a chantilly center topped with vanilla-flavored chestnut cream. The quantities of sugar and vanilla must be administered with scientific precision so that the chestnut cream is not too rich. It was invented by an Austrian confectioner, Antoine Rumpelmeyer. In 1903, he founded Angelina, the famous *salon de thé* beloved of Coco Chanel and Marcel Proust, opposite the Tuileries gardens in Paris. Neither the *salon* nor the recipe has changed to this day. The cake, whose chestnut purée is piped in lines close to one another, although no visual show-stopper, is an intriguing sight. To conquer the Mont Blanc, be it the highest peak in Europe or the dessert, involves strategic planning. It is almost a shame to ruin the harmoniously assembled structure whose recipe no doubt includes some secret: the happiness it procures seems to derive from a magic potion. Meringue lovers are familiar with the traditional *polonaise*, a cake whose heyday is long gone and that is hard to find today. The story goes that the *polonaise* was made with brioches that went unsold but that the pastry chefs were loath to throw out. They soaked them with kirsch, spread them with pastry cream, covered the whole cake with meringue, then garnished them with candied fruits. Today, there are few pastry chefs who still offer us the opportunity to taste this cake of yesteryear. It is still sought after by its fans and it would be worthwhile updating it. It is light and airy, but only a master pastry chef can turn it into an exceptionally good cake.

The use of meringue is not solely the preserve of desserts of times past. It has continued to inspire major contemporary pastry chefs such as Gaston Lenôtre, who, in the 1950s, created his Succès (Success)

layer cake. This comprises two circles of almond meringue with a filling of attractive swirls of praline-flavored butter cream (the praline contains finely chopped caramel-coated almonds and hazelnuts). The sweet, rich cream highlights the subtle yet marked praline, which in turn plays up a meringue that is both crunchy and tender. Today, Pierre Hermé makes meringues with a center of mousseline cream, changing the flavors with the seasons. At his boutique, they are sold wrapped in colored cellophane like giant candies.

This overview of traditional cakes would be incomplete if we did not take a look at the charlotte and the *fraisier* (a sophisticated strawberry shortcake), cakes that are made in summer. Antonin Carême, a famous nineteenth-century chef who worked for the French statesman Charles Maurice de Talleyrand-Périgord, was the inventor of the Parisian charlotte. It was his idea to line a mold with ladyfingers and to fill it with a fruit cream or mousse, garnished with the same fresh fruits. Strawberries, raspberries, and pears are ideal, as is the passion fruit. The *fraisier* is just as delicate and refreshing. Parisian pastry chefs are specialists in this particular dessert. The particularly light type of sponge, invented by Auguste Jullien in the twentieth century when he removed the almonds from the Genovese loaf, and its fluffy mousseline cream, on which are set tight rows of fresh, tasty strawberries, make this cake an appropriate summer treat. It is topped with a thin layer of marzipan fondant, as shiny as a white mirror. The *fraisier*, which can easily be made on a grander scale, is a dessert that is perfect for parties, and is indeed often served on festive occasions.

Traditional desserts, we have seen, tell stories that often become part of family lore. They accompany important occasions in our lives, bringing a sweet gentleness that delights successive generations of gourmands. And this is how these highlights of Sunday lunches, birthday dinners, and holiday celebrations have crossed the centuries. Today, revisited by the new generation of pastry chefs, these time-honored desserts have been modernized, enriching time-honored traditions.

MARLETTI
Sober, contemporary lines allow the perfectly constructed, seductive cakes to take pride of place at Marletti's (above center), from the traditional mille-feuille (facing page) to the revamped Paris-Brest (above left) and cream-filled choux pastry (above right), whose crunchy case accentuates the delicately flavored cream.

BERTHILLON

In the best tradition, yet surprisingly moist and substantial, here is the generous tarte Tatin that Muriel, granddaughter of Berthillon's founder, prepares for the cosy *salon de thé* next to the ice-cream store. The recipe is secret, but every day Muriel turns her tart out of the mold, anxious to see whether the caramel is not too dark, not too light, but just right. Order her large tarts and you'll have twelve happy guests.

Chocolate Magic

Eclairs, Mille-Feuilles, and Melt-in-the-Mouth Chocolate Cakes

STOHRER

A cake from Germany and the eastern part of France, the Black Forest, in Stohrer's inimitable style: the Amarena cherries nestle in a layer of chantilly cream, sandwiched between two layers of dark chocolate sponge (page 57).

JEAN-PAUL HÉVIN

"I set the mille-feuille on its side just before I eat it. That way, not only do I better appreciate the balance between the amount of cream and the chocolate puff pastry, but I can cut it easily with a fork and not crush it too much," says Jean-Paul Hévin (facing page). At long last, here is the answer to the delicate question: is there an elegant way to eat a mille-feuille?

The mere mention of the word "chocolate" has the power to make time stand still; bring a chocolate cake out and it will elicit a storm of reactions—of sight, taste, and smell. It is a phenomenon well known to chocolate lovers and chocoholics. It all starts with the almost hypnotic state induced by the sight of a chocolaty delight. The object of desire is always a feast for the eyes; we put off eating it, simply because we know that the pleasure will sooner or later come to an end. So there we are, in troubling expectation: should we destroy this harmonious creation? We anticipate the moment when we dig into the soft sponge and velvety cream to hear the rustling, crackling, and murmuring as textures come into contact, exuding a bouquet of chocolate aromas. So we wait, cake poised halfway between the plate and our lips. We take the time to appreciate the splendid architecture of the creation. We wait, and now close our eyes as we allow the fragrances of the bouquet to waft into our nostrils, the marriages of cacaos from Venezuela, Mexico, and Madagascar. We sniff out the Bourbon vanilla, whose suavity softens their bitterness. When we can wait no longer, we bring it to our lips, and then into our mouths. At last we savor the flavors that explode on our palate like fireworks. The crunchy, creamy, and meringue textures intermingle and dance, providing such sheer pleasure that we wish it would go on for ever.

Chocolate is close to the divine, it dallies with the forbidden, and it loves a secret. Unlike alcohol, it requires no company, and one can be joyfully solitary to savor it. Chocolate takes us on a very personal journey, somewhat like that of the opium smokers of yesteryear—minus the danger, of course. In fact, on the contrary; today's great pastry chefs have acquired such a fine mastery of chocolate that their cakes provide remarkably healthy benefits for both the body and soul. Chocolate is spellbinding, bewitching—quite magical. It has always been this way, ever since the Mayas cultivated it and the Aztecs paid homage to their gods with chocolate elixir. The drink comprised cacao laced with musk, cinnamon, pepper, chili, and vanilla. The only earthly creatures entitled to sip the divine drink were those

JEAN-PAUL HÉVIN

Jean-Paul Hévin's boutiques reflect his liking for style and things modern. The dark wood harmonizes perfectly with the various shades of the chocolate. His windows display all the specialties in both individual portions and sizes to share (page 61). We have a special weakness for the light, fresh Matcha and the bergamot-flavored Bergam. Safi is a Moroccan town renowned for its oranges, which flavor this cake, a tender combination of chocolate sponge and creamy chocolate mousse with bitter orange (above right). Less classic is the Violette: under a dark chocolate glaze lie melting layers of redcurrant- and violet-flavored chocolate mousse (above left). The Chocolat Framboise alternates chocolate mousse and raspberry-flavored cacao sponge (facing page).

who had received divine powers. When Emperor Montezuma received Hernán Cortés, he believed he was the reincarnation of the god Quetzalcóatl, whose coming had been announced by the oracles. He served him a bitter cocoa-bean drink called *xocoatl*. The conquistador was immediately won over by the sacred drink, and he brought back not only the cocoa beans, but also the recipe, for his king, Charles V. That is how chocolate reached the court of Spain in 1528. No sooner was it tasted than it became all the rage. The recipe for the nectar of the Aztec gods was simplified and adapted to European tastes: the vanilla, cinnamon, and black pepper were retained, and honey or sugar were added to sweeten it.

It was soon adopted in the rest of Europe, where it became equally popular. In fact, it was more than popular, attributed with virtues of all sorts, both nutritional and digestive, as well as evils of all sorts. It was even considered an aphrodisiac. Madame de Sévigné, a great correspondent of the seventeenth century, a witty, intelligent person who enjoyed the odd mocking comment, said to those for whom she had little respect, "Take chocolate in order that even the most tiresome company seems acceptable to you." One might wonder whether it is because there are still so many people of "tiresome company" that chocolate has extended its hold into every single country in Europe and much of the rest of the world. There are few who could go without it, particularly since the twentieth century. Because of its considerable cost and complicated preparation, cacao was a foodstuff reserved for royalty and the highest nobility. It was used very sparingly, in only a few desserts. Massaliot, a famous eighteenth-century writer of cookbooks, explained, in *Nouvelle instruction for confitures* (New Instructions for Preserves), how to make small cakes and marzipan using chocolate. He reveals his secrets for flavoring genoise and other sponges, thus taking chocolate out of the apothecary's boutique and leading it gently into the kitchen. With a soaring demand for cacao, cacao trees were introduced onto the island of Martinique for cultivation, making the precious product more accessible. Pastry chefs rejoiced: cacao was now

CARETTE

Here's a large cake for chocolate macaroon fans to share with family or friends. A powerful but creamy black chocolate ganache is caught between two chocolate macaroon shells. Only a few pastry chefs are skilled enough to bake them so that they turn out just right. In a multitiered version, this would be the ideal cake to serve at the wedding of two chocoholics.

PIERRE HERMÉ

Pure, sober design and intense, vivid colors make up the setting designed by Christian Biecher for the boutique on Rue de Vaugirard (above and page 69). Pierre Hermé ceaselessly creates new cakes for every month of the year. For a few weeks, he makes variations on the Saint Honoré, which demands the greatest skills of pastry chefs, in the most varied range of flavors. Here, the Carrément Chocolat with airy dark chocolate cream harmonizes with the full-bodied caramelized choux pastries (facing page). The Plénitude (page 68), on the other hand, is available all year round. Its dome shelters a creamy center with bitter chocolate mousse and dark chocolate ganache.

available year-round and they explored the avenues it opened up to them for splendid creations.

The first true chocolate cake, as we know it, saw the light of day in 1832. Franz Sacher, pastry chef to Prince Metternich of Austria, created it in Austria for some high-ranking guests. The Sacher torte is a chocolate sponge with a filling of apricot preserve, glazed with black chocolate icing over a covering of the same apricot preserve which ensures relatively long-lasting freshness. From that momentous meal on, anything in the realm of chocolate cake production seemed possible, including some quite sublime cakes. The great pastry chefs of Paris experimented endlessly with ganaches, fondants, and mousses using the pure criollo (a rare, fine-flavor bean) and *grands crus*—in which all the beans come from the same region—from Mexico, Nicaragua, Venezuela, and Colombia. They added zing with spices, freshness with fruits, suavity with vanilla—a stunning range of flavors whose sole aim was to bring pleasure, adding to the intrinsic virtues of chocolate.

The first truly audacious chocolate cake of the twentieth century was made by Cyriaque Gavillon in 1955. Several years previously, he had bought the famous Maison Dalloyau, which ever since has been making the famous, timeless Opéra: a triple layer of chocolate sponge gently soaked in strong coffee, separated by a mocha cream and then by a chocolate ganache. The shiny glazing, also of chocolate, is decorated with delicate gold leaf. The Opéra was a revolution in both taste and aesthetics, and was copied far and wide with varying degrees of success. It is an explosion on the palate, with just one mouthful revealing a wide range of flavors and textures that come together in daring, yet perfect, harmony.

Another classic that was a complete innovation when it was made in the 1960s is La Feuille d'Automne (Autumn Leaf) by Gaston Lenôtre. The celebrated pastry chef put together something quite different from the traditional chocolate cakes, heavy in content and structure. With his Feuille d'Automne, a light, beautiful dessert was born. A corolla of attractively scalloped delicate leaves of chocolate top a light cake comprising meringue, mousse, and chocolate ganache. Gaston Lenôtre transformed chocolate into a delicate foodstuff—something to be savored rather than devoured. This was a turning point: chocolate emerged from the world of childhood to become a foodstuff adults could enjoy.

More than ever over the past few years, chocolate lovers have become increasingly devoted. There are those who favor bitterness or fruity aromas, those who seek out full-bodied flavors, and those who appreciate mildness. Until recently, most people went for dark chocolate; today there is a swing back to the milk chocolate we enjoyed as children. However, whether chocolate is dark, milk,

intense, or delicate, whenever it is part of a cake, it adds its own special dimension and makes it all the more irresistible.

For chocoholics and lovers of chocolate cake, the ultimate place to go is the appropriately named La Maison du Chocolat, (The House of Chocolate). For over thirty years, the company has enjoyed remarkable success in Paris, New York, Tokyo, London, Sydney, Hong Kong, and Montreal. Founded by Robert Linxe, the first boutique, dedicated solely to chocolate, was an innovation in the 1970s. Shops that sold only chocolate were few and far between at the time, for in France chocolate was eaten principally at Christmas and Easter. This institution focuses on producing simply sublime products. Robert Linxe was soon named—and justifiably so—as "the wizard of ganache." Ganache is a subtle combination of chocolate and crème fraîche, in which the slightly sour notes of cream sharpen the powerful aromas of chocolate. Linxe was the first to flavor his ganaches, making them quite irresistible. He added lemon, mint, and caramel with salted butter. It was this last ingredient—an immediate hit—that gave him the idea for his cake, the Rigoletto. Then the delicious Marroni ganache led him to create the tart that bears the same name, found in his shop only in the winter. It uses the best marrons glacés from Italy. Robert Linxe creates his cakes, working as a chocolate maker does: he seeks simple recipes that highlight the strength of his primary ingredients. He collaborates with Valrhona, the chocolate maker, selecting their best *crus*, to create his own couverture chocolate. The chocolate tart, the supreme classic of La Maison du Chocolat, is an outstanding example that embodies the image that Robert Linxe has always tried to convey of the soberness, quality, and refinement of his establishment. Elegance and pure graphic lines are *de rigueur*. A plain, creamy ganache is spread over a delicate sweet crust that highlights the full range of aromas of a *grand cru* cacao. The flavors and the contrast between the crumbly crust and melting cream are sheer delight to all chocolate lovers.

GÉRARD MULOT
This pastry shop has an attractive front opening onto the Rue Tournon near Saint Sulpice church (above, center). Its Cœur Frivole (Frivolous Heart) is named to suggest the lightness of the two types of chocolate mousse, milk and dark, for purists seeking out an all-chocolate dessert (facing page). The assembly of chocolate, blackberry, and a hybrid of blackberry and raspberry (above left) is more off the beaten path, as is the pistachio bavarois (above right).

AOKI
The molten chocolate cake: under a firm exterior lies a liquid chocolate heart that is at its best after a few seconds in the microwave oven (pages 72–73).

LA MAISON DU CHOCOLAT
The chocolate tart is a great classic: the shortcrust pastry is extremely delicate and the chocolate cream is divinely unctuous (above left). Contemporary creations, such as the Rigoletto, which brings together chocolate and caramel on a sweet crust (above right), and the Brésilien (Brazilian) (above center and facing page), with its creamy mousse and chocolate sponge, will be a hit with coffee lovers. The chocolate éclair, probably the all-time best-seller in all pastry shops, with its soft choux pastry, its chocolate pastry cream, and its shiny dark chocolate glaze, is for purists (pages 76–77).

The tart is as irresistible as the caramel éclairs, another creation by Robert Linxe, who brought status to a flavor hitherto relegated to the sidelines. Eclairs must be sold and eaten very shortly after they are made, for the choux pastry is truly delicious only for a short time after it is prepared. At La Maison du Chocolat, therefore, éclairs can only be bought on weekdays. But whatever the day, it would be foolish to resist the temptation of the outstanding chocolate concoctions. Why not try a Salvador, with its raspberry pulp, whose sour notes heighten the powerfully flavored truffle mousse? Next, taste an all-chocolate Délice—sponge, almond cream, and icing—or a Pleyel, soft chocolate cake and almonds. The Rigoletto is a must: the sweet, butter-flavored sugar crust with just a touch of salt is followed by mouth-melting chocolate sponge and caramel mousse. The cake is a veritable concerto in chocolate major. A few years ago, Gilles Marchal took over this venerable institution, and without modifying the traditions he has begun adding sparkle to the dessert menu of certain luxury hotels. He is one of the professionals working toward making Paris the world capital of sweets, and of chocolate in particular, once again.

"The pleasure that chocolate offers and elicits is immediate, absolute, and incomparable. It evokes childhood and crystallizes memories for the future. It should never be betrayed." So says another wizard of chocolate, Jean-Paul Hévin, an unpredictable, irresistible man who defies description. Even if we add the words "mischievous," "facetious," and "winning," the portrait would not be quite complete. He is reserved, but if you catch his eye (forget-me-not blue), you cannot fail to notice his piercing look that reveals a mathematical sense of precision—the kind of precision necessary for the chemistry that he uses with devastating ease in his chocolate making. It is a look that goes right to the soul. Monsieur Hévin measures, weighs, combines, and distils the *grands crus* of cacao, spices, flavors, and textures as no one else does. It is his lifetime's work. His Pyramide, an eye-catching technical creation that pays tribute to the Louvre pyramid by I. M. Pei, just a short distance away from the chocolate shop, sends one

into a state of bliss. It has multiple layers of alternating cacao sponge with almond paste and bitter ganache. It is an exploration in the extremes of chocolate. The Ecuador, now a classic, alternates *dacquoise* pastry, meringue, and very bitter chocolate mousse, entirely covered by a thin layer of milk chocolate. The confrontation of textures—the crumbly meringue, the creamy mousse, and the crunchy glaze—and the marriage of mild and strong tastes makes for a somewhat disconcerting taste experience, both exciting and greatly amusing. The Safi is a hymn to the town of the same name. The country of Morocco can be proud of it. The Safi combines a slightly bitter chocolate sponge with a creamy chocolate and orange mousse—three layers of each. How can one not adore it unconditionally? And what

LENÔTRE
The Opéra is the great classic that never fails to please. Under a fine layer of black chocolate are layers of soft sponge, coffee butter cream, and truffle paste or ganache (above). A meringue filled with chocolate mousse lies hidden under these delicately frilled leaves. Feuille d'Automne is another of Gaston Lenôtre's great classics (facing page).

is there to say of the old-fashioned chocolate macaroon with its generous filling? No words are adequate. When your plate has been cleaned, you will probably feel as you do when you close an exceptionally moving book. What a shame to have finished it already, to no longer be in the thick of the plot. How sad it is to bid farewell to this spellbinding universe, full of humor, tenderness, and passion.

The Maison Hévin creations radiate simplicity. No doubt this is why Monsieur Hévin has such a following in Japan. This likable personality enjoys, above all, surprising people and making them happy. He works hard to send our senses into a frenzy—with the scents of chocolate, they are awakened with surprising ease and speed. Monsieur Hévin clearly makes chocolate cakes for love of his fellow humans. He was awarded the title of *Meilleur Ouvrier de France* (Best Craftsman of France)—no mean feat—in a competition that demands commitment, skill, and dedication. His science is that of a cacao specialist; his artistry reaches great heights; to all this, he adds an irrepressible joie de vivre. He never says no to a challenge, and for Epiphany, he audaciously breaks with time-honored traditions by making a *galette des rois* filled with chocolate. Even the puff pastry is made with cacao butter, giving it a dark amber color, irresistibly beautiful. The chocolate almond cream melts in the mouth—a revelatory taste sensation. Say nothing while you savor this miraculous creation: words are inadequate and will only detract from the exceptional experience. If you are lucky enough to taste this *galette* you will fall victim to its magic. Beware: it appears only in January, and you will have to wait an entire year for the miracle to reoccur. This is torture for those who can't get it out of their minds.

Another famous chocolate maker and pastry chef is Pierre Hermé. He has just opened a boutique devoted entirely to his chocolates and macaroons. However, if you want to taste his chocolate cakes, you will have to go to his two other pastry shops. There you will find, nestling among the other

astonishing creations, the Carrément Chocolat (Definitely Chocolate, or Squarely Chocolate), the Mogador, and the Cerise sur le Gâteau (Cherry on the Cake). It is impossible to talk of the cakes made by the king of French patisserie, and no doubt his title could be extended to the known universe, using anything but superlatives—entirely justified, it should be said. Let us start with the Carrément Chocolat, a somewhat secretive cake. People should take their time over eating it. It is cut as straight as a die—a perfect square—and covered with glossy black chocolate. The creator calls the sponge "soft"; the cream is velvety; there is a crunch to it and the fine leaves are crisp. All this goes to make up a pure, sober, intense, mysterious chocolate experience. The individual textures impose

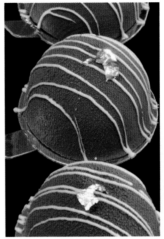

their differences but come together to create new, unexpected textures. You may well have a second helping to understand what goes into the making of the cake, but you will soon give up. Carrément Chocolat is part of a perfect world, made not to be understood, but to be adored, to seduce, and to intoxicate. The Mogador puts on a different show—not surprising, since it bears the name of a well-known Parisian theater. This is both a taste sensation and a spectacle that is pleasing on the eye. In order of appearance: a chocolate macaroon base, a milk chocolate ganache, and whipped cream on which passion fruits and caramelized roasted pineapples dance. Another cake for lovers of dark chocolate is the Plénitude (Fullness). As much a candy as a cake, the bitter chocolate aromas of the mousse and the ganache combine subtly with the aromas of the caramel. The square shards of chocolate that rest delicately on the shiny dome give this cake the appearance of a contemporary jewel. Indeed, Pierre Hermé considers aesthetics to be as important as taste; after all, it enhances the pleasure of the tasting experience. He is not without humor: on top of the stylish, shapely Cerise sur le Gâteau perches…a cherry. Cerise sur le Gâteau is an ode to milk chocolate, an enthusiastic homage to Daniel Peter, to whom we are indebted for the invention of milk chocolate in 1875. The cake comprises a *dacquoise* with crunchy hazelnuts, hazelnut crisp, thin wafers of milk chocolate, and milk chocolate ganache and milk chocolate chantilly. Once it has touched your tongue, this cake will perform the dance of the seven veils on your palate. It is a cake to take one's time over as you try to keep your feet on the ground. If you let yourself be carried away, addiction awaits you. Take a look at the lines outside Pierre Hermé's shops and you will realize just how many have succumbed to temptation.

In terms of chocolate cakes, Paris has many surprises tucked away. Each great pastry chef makes his or her special chocolate dessert. Then it is up to you to stumble across it when exploring the city,

PAIN DE SUCRE

As we talk of *haute couture*, we can talk of *haute pâtisserie*. The pastry chefs here like nothing better than constant reinvention, the better to take their faithful clients' palates by surprise. For Easter, they put together this beautiful dome filled with a citrus cream and a dark chocolate mousse, topped with a gold-leaf sugar egg (facing page).

MARLETTI

Exquisite flavors fan out in the display case (above right). Marletti's innovations are a perfect balance between textures and flavors, as in this ephemeral creation of dark and milk chocolate with caramel cream (above left). Both traditional pastry lovers and more adventurous souls seeking out new combinations will be seduced.

hear about it by word of mouth, or get a bee in your bonnet about what you really want. Fashionistas, even though they might be keeping an eye on their weight, give in when shopping becomes just too stressful to bear and head for a stylish *salon de thé*. At the Grande Epicerie of the Bon Marché department store on the Left Bank, the appropriately named Le Gâteau is an impressively high creation in which alternate pistachio crisp, a compote of raspberries with balsamic vinegar, gianduja cream, and dark chocolate mousse, all repeated several times and encased in a chocolate coffer. The Tonka, named for a spice little used until today, is more classic: it subtly combines chocolate mouse with vanilla mousse.

Fabrice Le Bourdat, former head pastry chef at the Martinez Hotel, Cannes, the Bristol in Paris, and other luxury hotels, has brought the traditional alliance of vanilla and chocolate to perfection in one of his gateaux, the Vollon, available in his small boutique Blé Sucré in the twelfth arrondissement of Paris, near the Place de la Bastille. The Vollon is a dark brown dome that reflects the surrounding lights. It is composed of a fluffy almond *dacquoise*, a vanilla cream, a crisp praline pastry, and a zabaglione with an intense chocolate flavor. Le Bourdat has succeeded in creating a pastry that is both magnificent and subtle. On eating the cake, one is stunned by the complexity of its architecture—a small jewel that has both refinement and grandeur.

At the end of the picturesque and lively market street, Rue Mouffetard, Carl Marletti has set up a pastry shop. Until recently, he was the head pastry chef at the Grand Hotel Intercontinental in Paris, where people flocked for his outstanding mille-feuilles. They are now available in his boutique, but it is the Censier that you should sample. A base of chocolate popped rice supports a scoop of velvety, melt-in-your-mouth chocolate cream that offers a striking contrast to the crackles as you eat the rice. It is a truly fun pastry.

If you have fond memories of the Black Forest cake you ate as a child, you will find a faithful recreation in Les Halles neighborhood, on Rue Montorgueil, another busy market street, at Stohrer. Any gourmand worthy of the name will cross Paris to find pastry that meets their exacting standards. A merely average Black Forest cake just will not do. Stohrer's meets all the criteria for excellence: the chocolate mousse and sponge, the whipped cream, and the kirsch-soaked cherries all revive emotions that go back many years, emotions that are both sensual and reassuring, in a moment that one wishes would last forever.

LAURENT DUCHÊNE
An attractive boutique located in the charming neighborhood of Butte aux Cailles (above). Chocoholics come for the molten chocolate cakes, with a liquid chocolate center hidden well below a dusting of confectioners' sugar, as well as for the house specialty, La Butte (page 82), a pairing of chocolate and caramel. Among the cakes with fruit, there is the Ambroisie, with raspberry ganache, and the original, utterly delicious Equinoxe with coriander-flavored ganache (page 83).

BERTHILLON
The famed ice-cream maker of Ile Saint-Louis has opened a charming *salon de thé*, the size of a refined boudoir (page 87). Seated at its marble tables, you can enjoy the classic brownie with Grenoble walnuts—simply divine with genuine vanilla ice cream (page 86).

There is a repertoire of classical chocolate cakes; pastry chefs, as we have seen, also like to innovate. One of the latest and most significant creations in chocolate cakes has been made not by a pastry chef, but by a great chef, Michel Bras, who was awarded three Michelin stars. After working on a most unusual cake for two years, in 1981 an all-cacao cake appeared on his menu. At its core is a practically liquid texture of pure chocolate that gives this cake its name: the Coulant (Liquefied). It is served straight out of the oven to the surprise and delight of the clients at his restaurant. As soon as they dip their spoons into the little cake, they discover the runny, hot liquid that exudes the full range of powerful chocolate aromas. It is truly irresistible.

The Coulant was so successful that innumerable pastry chefs have made adaptations of it. Its popularity has extended to the English-speaking world, where different versions go under the names of fondant, *moelleux* (moist), and *mi-cuit* (half-baked). The idea is essentially the same: the interior of the cake is either very soft, or even runny, particularly if it is baked in the microwave at home for a few minutes, as pastry chefs sometimes advise. In actual fact, the fondant is a classic chocolate cake baked at low temperature, which is what gives it its distinctive texture. It is generally served with whipped cream or custard. The *moelleux au chocolat* (often called a molten or lava chocolate cake) is runny inside and has a well-baked crust. The texture of the *mi-cuit* is soft and very dense. Whatever the style of this relatively new chocolate cake, is has brought to gourmands the satisfaction of the cake that is the ultimate in chocolate.

Beyond trends and fashions, chocolate will always remain a source of intense pleasure for those who eat it, and a magical product for those who work with it and who seek endlessly to overcome its strong character and bring out its flavors through new combinations.

**LA GRANDE EPICERIE
DU BON MARCHÉ**
At the entrance to the food hall of this store, in the midst of the pastry counter, chocolate cakes draw all eyes towards them, so tempting are they (above right). The amazing cube called, quite simply, Le Gâteau (The Cake), alternates pistachio sponge, jellied raspberry, and a gianduja cream (facing page). Another interesting creation is the Tonka, with the vanilla flavors of ylang-ylang and Tonka bean (above left, in family size, and pages 90–91, individual cakes).

Contemporary Creations

Macaroons, *Verrines*, and Caramel

PAIN DE SUCRE
With the introduction of
verrines, little glasses, pastry
chefs have created a new
range of desserts that mingle
flavors and textures in
astonishing combinations
(page 93). With their new
flavors, like elderberry
blossom and pistachio-cherry,
macaroons seduce everyone
(facing page).

FAUCHON
The array of éclairs here
comprises so many original
flavors that it surprises
anyone who goes into the
shop. Instead of the classic
glaze, the coffee éclairs have
a fine layer of white
chocolate printed with a
leopard skin motif (page 96).
The eyes of Mona Lisa follow
you from the dark chocolate
topping of the milk chocolate
éclairs (page 97).

Today, in Paris, pastry chefs are outdoing themselves—and one another—as they display their talents, inventiveness, skills, and refined audacity to give our blasé palates a wake-up call, amaze our disoriented taste buds, and astound our eyes, accustomed to daily sightings of overkill. They know their classics inside out, back to front, and by heart, and although their traditional desserts are perfection itself, thanks to their masterly techniques, they take inspiration in whimsy and let their virtuoso imagination run free.

What is striking about those who are known as "great" pastry chefs (the mere mention of their names sets connoisseurs' mouths watering) is how they shatter well-established codes. Their bold inventiveness is similar to that of painters, the only significant difference being that their creations are more acquirable—and a good thing too, because the art of pastry constantly piques our curiosity and appeals to our gourmandism.

The pastry chefs have tamed sugar and taken control of cream; they dispense just the right amount of butter and bring fruits onstage when least expected. They seek out the best ingredients, use only natural colorings, and their ephemeral sweetnesses have proved that cakes are no longer the anathema they were twenty or thirty years ago. What remains in these desserts is the spirit of sugar; an ethereal element abounds in the cakes, creams, and mousses. The tangy and spicy notes form a symphony whose music resounds lastingly on our palates and in our memories. Impeccable technique is displayed at every stage of cake making. Pastry chefs give us the best of what they have received, and indeed the best of themselves. They go out of their way to bring pleasure to others, to those true gourmands among us who justly appreciate the gift.

When we marvel at the works of these creators, some of whom have been named *Meilleur Ouvrier de France* or the world's best pastry chef, we cannot fail to appreciate their sense of fantasy—sometimes even their humor—as well as their sophistication, perfection, and beauty; all the

PIERRE HERMÉ
Pierre Hermé's Ispahan
range, which associates rose,
raspberry, and litchi, is
irresistible (facing page). For
Valentine's Day, Ispahan is
made in a heart shape (above
right). The attractively
designed boutique on the
Rue de Vaugirard near
Montparnasse Station is
always filled with newly
created pastries (above left).

qualities that go to make up luxury. We may sometimes hesitate to bite into a cake, so unbelievable does it seem, but in the end we always succumb. The first mouthful opens the gateway to sheer happiness. Both the presentation and the composition are works of art that we first enjoy with our eyes before their flavors erupt and their textures dumbfound us. Crunchiness will have us astounded, softness will bind us in its spell, and a dash of creaminess will be the last sublime touch. Here we have consummate mastery distilled with measure and a little craziness, implemented with the greatest rigor. It is high art. A gang of dangerously seductive men and women exert their powers over people strolling through Paris. Saunter through the streets at your own risk: you may become addicted to a delectable creation at any moment, for they have set up shop throughout the City of Lights.

They present their seasonal collections in the manner of *haute couturiers*, sometimes calling on the seasons of far-flung regions to widen the range of surprises in store for us. Color plays a major role, no longer restrained to creamy or chocolaty hues. The sharp tints of fruits and flowers might add exotic touches. Already extremely refined, these cakes satisfy the palates of connoisseurs seeking new sensations and new flavors.

Certain trends are discernible in the midst of this ever-increasing crescendo of high notes and delicately sweet arias. Filled almond macaroons are here, there, and everywhere. Caramel in all its forms is omnipresent. The most exotic fruits are to be seen in every neighborhood. Little glasses—*verrines*—hold multicolored, miniature desserts.

The prevailing fantasy, humor, and joyfulness that characterize contemporary desserts are found, first and foremost, in the macaroon, now a must. Gourmets in a hurry adore them, because they can be downed while on the go. Small enough to be eaten like chocolates and cherries (with the same caveat: once you start, it's difficult to stop), they are available in a practically infinite range of flavors,

from the classic to the zany; fruity, flowery, and even bizarre, resulting in colors that are sometimes as vivid as children's candies. Try out the tastes you know and love; test the disconcertingly unexpected flavors that you may even loathe—who knows, the macaroon is so temptingly delightful that it may magically make you change your mind. It has become so chic, so trendy, that a beautiful box of macaroons is now the perfect hostess gift, outranking even chocolates and flowers.

Almond macaroons are not a recent invention. They have been eaten in many regions of France since the Middle Ages. Then, they were smooth disks made of egg white, beaten with sugar and blanched, ground almonds. The baking method had to ensure that the crisp crust retained a soft interior. The macaroon widely eaten today, also known as the Gerbet macaroon or the *macaron*, differs not in its texture but in its presentation. It was created in Paris late in the nineteenth century, when a certain Monsieur Gerbet decided to put two of the biscuit-like confections together with a ganache. Vanilla, chocolate, coffee, raspberry, and pistachio were the flavors. The bite-sized treat was born, and success was already on the horizon. Today, the ganache has been lightened and the garnishes range from delicate pastels to shades we could barely even imagine as edible. There are showcases with rows of flashy green lime with basil, amaretto cherry red, the deep yellowy-orange of mangoes, and the aniseed-flavored turquoise of sparkling sunny seas. Black licorice has practically become a classic.

In the world of macaroons, Pierre Hermé reigns supreme. He has concocted new forms of the madeleine that no longer bring back memories of childhood, but rather memories of adulthood, evoking travels, a special atmosphere, a landscape, or a special emotion, languid or sensual. Hermé has introduced the outrageous and bizarre into his creations, harmonizing flavors, aromas, textures, and colors. He has perfect control over the pairings, coming within a hair's breadth of dissonance and then veering away from it at the last moment. You have to be either one of the initiated, or follow your

PIERRE HERMÉ
Two of Pierre Hermé's major hits, the Infiniment Vanille, in which vanillas from Tahiti, Mexico, and Madagascar are combined, and the coffee tart (facing page). The macaroons are produced in a large range of subtle juxtapositions, such as wasabi cream and candied grapefruit (above left), and more traditional flavors, like the pure Venezuelan chocolate (above right). The seasonal macaroons make up a rainbow of colors in the boutique that sells only these confections (page 103). Rose and caramel with salted butter are perennials, but the Mogador is a modern creation comprising passion fruit and milk chocolate (page 102).

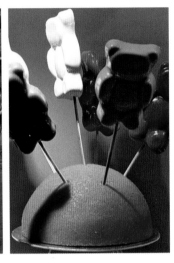

PLAZA ATHÉNÉE

If you want to sample one of the most delicious *religieuses* with caramel with salted butter, take tea at the Plaza Athénée hotel. In addition to this classic from the pastry repertory, Christophe Michalak offers fun creations such as the Flower Power, a *financier* topped with a flower of colored chantilly (above left), the Pomme d'Amour (Toffee Apple), with strawberry and violet mousse (above center), and the Bisounours (Care Bears) with marshmallow (above right).

LADURÉE

One of Ladurée's contemporary creations, the Baiser (Kiss), has a white chocolate shell, a soft coconut macaroon, and delicious exotic fruit compote—a most refreshing, light-hearted dessert (facing page).

gourmand's instinct in order to make your way through the universe of the macaroon—surreal, trendy, and a veritable passion in the city.

Mad for macaroons? Rush to another temple of the bite-sized delights: Ladurée, where the small confection is the signature product. How will you choose among the twenty or so flavors, each one more tempting than the next, lined up in a softly lit display case? Rose? Blackcurrant violet? Cherry? Orange blossom? Or the seasonal products, which vary from year to year, like mint or lily of the valley, bergamot, mango with jasmine? Or chestnut?

It's impossible to decide whether Ladurée's caramel with salted butter is superior to Pierre Hermé's Infiniment Caramel (Infinitely Caramel). One is divine; the other is heavenly. It's easy to make round trips between the Ladurée and Pierre Hermé boutiques. Both have stores on the Champs Elysées, at Saint Germain des Prés, and near the Madeleine Church. Gourmands and macaroon aficionados can thus have endless debates about the relative merits of each.

At Ladurée, pastry chef Philippe Andrieu presides over the enchanting range. Using the unchangeable classic as a base, he conducts his experiments—some become classics in their turn while others are available for just a season. The vanilla-vanilla macaroon is sheer delight. It is an assembly of three types of vanilla, from Madagascar, Mexico, and Tahiti, put together in the same way as a champagne. To taste this macaroon is to experience exceptional refinement. The three provenances are clearly recognizable, despite their infinitely small differences, and they explode in a bouquet of peppery, floral, woody harmonics, exotic, delightful, and enchanting. Another exhilarating experience comes with eating the caramel-apple macaroon, a portion you will not want to share. The two shells are caramel flavored, and they are sandwiched together with a delicate mousse, also caramel, with pieces of golden roasted apple that have retained just a little crunch. Philippe Andrieu

GÉRARD MULOT
Mulot's Amaryllis has become a great classic. It's a perfect harmony of crisp meringue, very light vanilla cream, and the tangy note of fresh raspberries.

**LA GRANDE EPICERIE
DU BON MARCHÉ**
In the brightly colored display
counters at the entrance to
the food hall, the cakes steal
the limelight (above left). The
Yuzu Mania is, without a
doubt, the most astonishing
and refined of them all. Its
core holds a lime mousse
and a velvety cream flavored
with yuzu, a small mandarin-
sized citrus fruit from Japan
(above right and facing page).

DES GÂTEAUX ET DU PAIN
This shiny dome, as white as
porcelain, is Claire Damon's
interpretation of cheesecake.
She pairs genuine
Philadelphia cream cheese,
specially imported, with a
delicious raspberry cream
(pages 110–111).

created it to evoke the apples his grandfather gently simmered over the fire in his house in south-west France. It is a perfect transcription of a simple pleasure, embodied in an exquisite pastry.

Macaroon folly is raging in Paris; not a single pastry maker in the city has escaped the trend. Chocolate makers, not content to offer the best of all-chocolate macaroons, have also got into the swing of things. Jean-Paul Hévin makes macaroons with violet and figs. However, there is one place that macaroon lovers should under no circumstances miss: Le Pain de Sucre, in the Marais district, a tiny boutique that belongs to Nathalie Robert and Didier Mathray. Although their range is not as extensive as Pierre Hermé's or Ladurée's, their creations definitely deserve top star rating. The delicate almond cookies and the cream fillings with fruit pulp turn their macaroons into instants of pure delight, in which the simplicity rivals the surprise they create. The moment you taste the delightful elderberry-blossom macaroon with chestnut honey, the refreshing pistachio-cherry, and the all-blackcurrant will be memorable; each bite leaves you feeling you have the flower or fruit in your mouth. For perfect happiness, however, a word to the wise: don't hold on to your macaroons till the next day, for they lose their slightly crisp yet tender texture.

The caramel with salted butter macaroon is unanimously acclaimed, perhaps because caramel has become the flavor of the moment, especially when accentuated by a few grains of sea salt. Caramel is cheekily making a place for itself, dethroning coffee and even chocolate. It is said to be a reminder of childhood; its smell is thought to be reassuring; it speaks to the nose as it does to the palate of sweetness and happiness. Even the most traditional desserts are being seduced by caramel. Savoring Christophe Michalak's caramel *religieuse* with salted butter at the Plaza Athénée Hotel will take you to the very top rung on the ladder of culinary delight. The gilt and marble of the Galerie des Gobelins will have practically no effect on you in comparison to your reaction when you taste the

voluptuous cream in a choux pastry that is crisp and tender at the same time. The last mouthful will take you to nirvana. And if you don't have a penchant for luxury hotels, go to Claire Damon's boutique. She was Michalak's longtime second-in-command, and her caramel *religieuse* with salted butter is perfect if you are longing for a blissful moment of gourmandism. Some of her clients have made this slightly offbeat *religieuse* part of their daily routine. Tarts are notoriously open to new ideas, and they have also taken on caramel with their usual generosity. Sadaharu Aoki's tart with its lovely spiral topping is delightfully refined, and proves that the Japanese chef established in Paris has mastered a taste typical of Brittany, whose signature candy is the caramel with salted butter.

Caramel has enabled contemporary desserts to showcase a flavor that until today has been on the sidelines. With fruits and flowers, pastries have revealed new tastes, often from faraway places. Their role is not to be underestimated, for they lighten the sugar content of creams, allowing us to increase our intake of cakes! Now, in Paris, next to the traditional apples, pears, strawberries, black-currants, and raspberries, you will find pineapple, coconut, litchi, passion fruit, and mango. Citrus fruits, including grapefruit and its small Japanese relative, the subtly flavored yuzu, have made a note-worthy entrance. Until recently, flowers were confined to candy; they now make their voices heard in pastry. Creams are fragrant with rose, violet, poppy, elderberry, and orange blossom, and indeed they seem to have gained some of the lightness of the floral perfumes. The new harmonies are daring, but once you have tasted them you will certainly by won over by the incredible finished product of these natural essences.

In 1998, Pierre Hermé invented his now celebrated creation, named Ispahan. It constituted a verita-ble revolution in the world of desserts, a clarion call. It was certainly bold to combine rose, raspberry, and litchi; in addition, it required his unsurpassed technique for this unlikely blend to appear so appropriate.

PAIN DE SUCRE
A couple of pastry chefs, Nathalie Robert and Didier Mathray, display, alongside their exquisite *viennoiseries*, creations that attain the level of high art and that vary with the seasons. Above, right and left, is the Bollywood, an unusual, mouth-watering marriage of curried pineapple pulp with a velvety cilantro cream. They are also constantly reinventing the éclair. Here we have one with passion fruit and salted butter caramel (above center). Now a classic of the boutique, the Ephémère (Ephemeral) is for lovers of coconut, here combined with a blackcurrant marmalade (facing page).

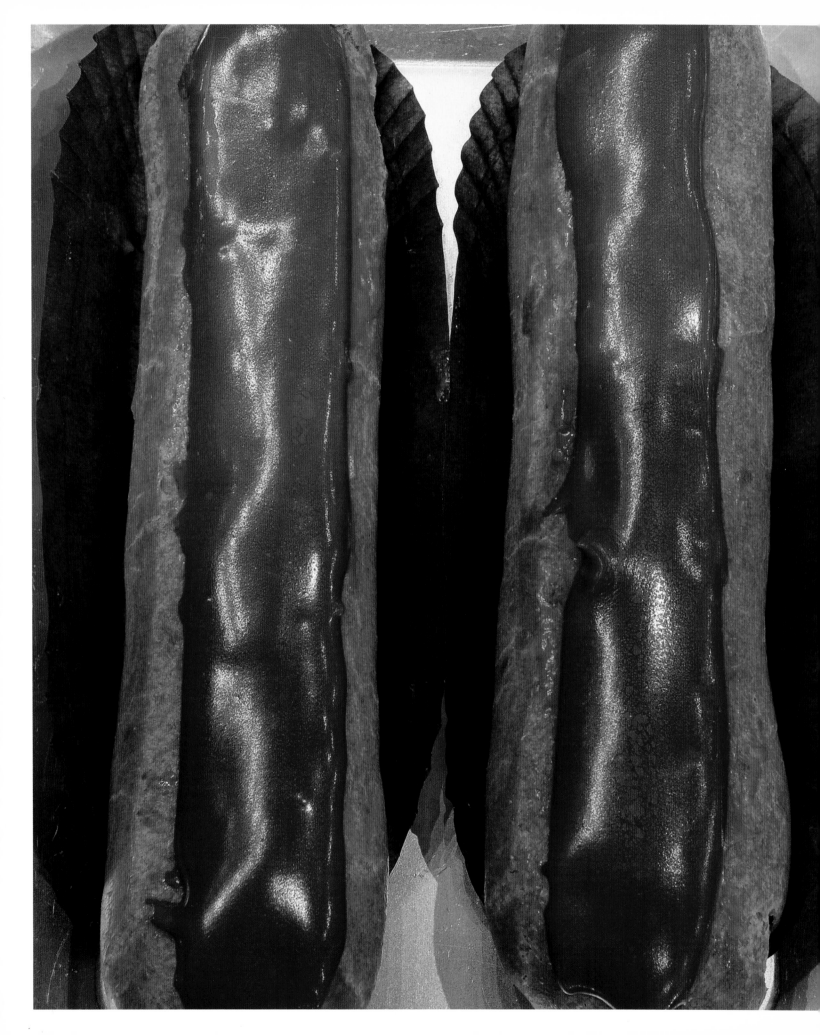

A white scoop topped with a sprig of blackcurrants, christened Ephémère (Ephemeral), comprises coconut meringue with just a hint of hazelnut, an interior of blackcurrent jelly, and an unctuous coconut cream. Eat it and you'll feel as if a tiny magician has waved his wand over your taste buds. Didier Mathray of Le Pain de Sucre is the creator of this marvel. For many years he was pastry chef with Pierre Gagnaire. In that Michelin three-starred restaurant, his "grand dessert" astounded the woman learning at his side, Nathalie Robert. She is equally qualified in pastry making; she is also Didier's wife. In their pretty little shop in the Marais district, the duo use their boundless imagination to create desserts that are aesthetically remarkable and unfailingly delectable. Miss Marple is a madeleine-type sponge made of chestnut flour, quince jelly, and chestnut cream. It is a sheer delight. They have transformed a classic: the éclair. Its shiny glaze has disappeared and become a paper-thin, lace-like, crackling veil that envelops it in a haze of crumble-type pastry, the same color as the fruit-flavored cream with which it is so generously garnished. This brings an entirely new consistency to the éclair, which is no longer merely bolted down but savored slowly: its textures and tastes are so intriguing, so seductive that no one can resist. Each éclair has a name. Lili is as yellow as the pineapple it is made of. It sits side by side with Clara, a lovely, rich brown with a pretty green ring that tells us it is made of chocolate with a mint infusion. It sets Petit Louis blushing with its raspberry and orange blossom water, but leaves another neighbor in salty butter caramel and passion fruit haughtily indifferent.

The traditional *religieuses* are also given a contemporary take, but they adapt better to flowers than to fruits. Ladurée makes rose-petal *religieuses*, as does Carl Marletti, and at the Plaza Athénée Hotel you will find them flavored with violet. Christophe Michalak gives his version an elegant topping; blackcurrants add a tangy note to the sensual cream, making the whole creation particularly piquant.

LA MAISON DU CHOCOLAT
Caramel is the undisputed star among the éclairs here. All Paris is crazy for them (page 114).

DES GÂTEAUX ET DU PAIN
Claire Damon's *religieuses* achieve a lightness unequaled anywhere. Here is one with unctuous caramel cream with fleur de sel, topped by a fondant icing (page 115).

LENÔTRE
In their latest *salon de thé*, near the new national library (above right), sample two of Gaston Lenôtre's creations that meet the requirements for both lightness and exotic flavors: the Plaisir (Pleasure), a vanilla and light chocolate mousse bavarois (above left) and the Schuss, a cream cheese mousse (facing page).

LAURENT DUCHÊNE
Here are up-to-date creations in an old-fashioned setting (above left): a little glass just made for caramel lovers (above right); a small, foamy strawberry slab that hides a light vanilla cream (above center); and the tangy Mikado, filled with a lime mousseline cream (facing page). The shop window of this chef is a symphony of colors, shapes, flavors, and textures that will satisfy all pastry lovers (pages 120–121).

Passion fruit has had a loyal following in Paris for over twenty years. It is now used more subtly, rigorously, and appropriately, the better to enhance its already heady, exotic aroma. Carl Marletti's Caraïbe (Caribbean) is a delicate milk-chocolate mousse with a creamy passion-fruit cream set on a crisp praline coconut base. It is light, refined, and surprising—in short, a delicious revelation.

The yuzu, a small citrus fruit from Japan whose flavor is somewhere between grapefruit and lemon—unless it is an elixir of both—is the downfall of gourmets. Of course being particularly trendy, it is expensive. At the Grande Epicerie de Paris food hall, which has one of the best pastry counters in the city, you will find a pastry called Yuzu; the Japanese flag ensures that no one mistakes its origins. It is an extraordinarily light sponge with a delicate yuzu-flavored cream, covered with a white fondant that is reminiscent of Mount Fuji. The top is stamped with red calligraphy worthy of an emperor's seal. It is an accomplishment.

Anyone with an adventurous palate, anyone ready to enjoy the tastes of far-flung places on the plate, ready to be spellbound by hitherto unknown flavors, should try Sadaharu Aoki's creations. You will not be disappointed when you succumb to the green and black beauty of Zen, a matcha tea cake with black sesame seeds. It would be foolish to try to resist its sweet, crisp pastry and velvety cream with black sesame. This crossbreed of a cake is hardly Zen-like, though: it upturns preconceptions and sends them flying. It is an unforgettable souvenir for lovers of the East. Aoki's range of macaroons does not neglect the more familiar, heady tastes of peach and violet, and will introduce you gently to the exotic flavors of yuzu and wasabi.

Another defining characteristic of today's desserts is the facility with which they snuggle into little shot glasses. There, they take on the appearance of an artist's palette, their colors superposed instead of spread out. You will eagerly dip a greedy teaspoon into these miniature marvels. Nathalie

Robert and Didier Mathray of Le Pain de Sucre make the finest *verrines*, as they are known, in Paris. In their shop window, they compose an array of colors and a magnificent superposition of textures. Their lists of ingredients may well be bewildering; not only is satisfaction guaranteed, but your hopes will be surpassed: you are certain to find them eminently more-ish. One comprises tangy apple pulp with cilantro, a sponge cake pastry, and a velvety pistachio cream. Another is a superposition of rice pudding and rhubarb. Yet another is made of coffee, whisky, barley water cream, and speculoos crumble.

Where did these *verrines* originate? Apparently it was the caterers who first had the idea. At buffets and receptions, they began serving light creamed vegetables in small glasses, as many finer restaurants do when they serve an *amuse-bouche*. The glasses were set out next to the canapés, and the transition from savory to sweet followed on logically. Restaurant-style desserts, adapted to fit into little glasses—easy to hold and eat from, convenient for cocktail parties—was the next step. Pastry chefs soon caught on to the idea: it is easy to combine textures and flavors in transparent glasses, and they dispense with the need for a crust to hold the creation together.

In Paris, cakes are like jewels displayed in fancy showcase windows. Our society may well be moving towards uniformity, but the best pastry chefs in the city are shifting the trend and creating a redeeming counter-current. To discover Paris through its pastry shops is a voyage of initiation comprised not of trials, but of moments of indescribable happiness that will remain in your memory.

SADAHARU AOKI
The Japanese pastry maker achieves perfect harmony between French *pâtisserie* and Japanese aesthetics. His caramel tart with salted butter has a sober design but is irresistibly tender (facing page). The rainbow of his macaroons reveals the exotic flavors of yuzu, matcha tea, and wasabi (above right), and the more classic tastes of violet, peach, and raspberry (above left). The bright yellow domes of praline and lemon, the soft green of matcha, and the pink of strawberry are displayed like jewels in the window (pages 124–125).

Viennoiseries and Treats To Go

Viennoiseries

—	Croissant	0,90€
—	Chocolatine	1,00€
—	Pain aux Raisins	1,10€
—	Roulé aux Amandes	1,30€
—	Chaussons Pommes	1,30€
—	Brioche Boule	1,00€
—	Tarte Caramel	1,10€
—	Tarte Framboises	1,10€
—	Paille D'Argent	1,50€
—	Pain Chocolat Blanc	1,10€
—	Viennoise	0,90€
—	Sachet de Madeleines	

Croissants, Loaves, and *Galettes*

SÉBASTIEN DÉGARDIN
Few people are familiar with the rich almond taste of the *pain de Gênes* (Genoa bread) that goes so well with a cup of tea (page 127). Sébastien Dégardin regaled his clients with it at the world-renowned Troisgros restaurant in Roanne, where he was pastry chef.

BLÉ SUCRÉ
This tiny boutique is chock-a-block full of finds for the gourmand. *Viennoiseries* take pride of place whatever the time of day: croissants, chocolate rolls, and almond rolls emerge from the oven with great frequency (facing page).

POILÂNE
There are few Parisians who are not familiar with Poîlane's pretty boutique on Rue du Cherche Midi in the sixth arrondissement. Its croissants, chocolate rolls, cinnamon-sprinkled apple tarts, and one of the best custard flans make an inviting display (page 131). In January, the *galette des rois* takes place of honor (page 130).

There is no better early morning activity in Paris than entering a good *boulangerie-pâtisserie*, where the delicate, smooth fragrance of butter wafting around will immediately give your sense of smell a friendly wake-up call. You will probably remain still for a few moments, spellbound by this gourmand's dream, right within your reach. All the perfectly golden, ready-to-eat Viennese-style pastries are there, exhaling their warm, heady odors. No matter how small they are, they are enough to set your stomach growling, even though you'd just stepped in for something small. You will be taken aback by a sudden desire to munch on those croissants, raisin rolls, apple turnovers, *palmiers*, and brioches, hot out of the baker's oven and known to the French as *"viennoiserie."* Where does the name come from?

The croissant, that iconic breakfast item, was invented in Vienna in 1683. The city was besieged by the Turkish Grand Vizier Kara Mustafa, but was finally freed thanks to a quick-thinking baker. According to legend, he was kneading his bread one night when he heard noises that he correctly interpreted as those of a tunnel being dug, which would have allowed the invader to penetrate Vienna. He sounded the alarm, foiled the plan, and saved his city. The quick-witted man was rewarded with a stock of flour that the invaders had left behind. To show appreciation for this gift and to celebrate the victory, he baked a pastry in the shape of the emblem of the Ottoman flag, a crescent—*"croissant"* in French. Princess Marie-Antoinette, when she came to France to marry the future king Louis XVI, brought the recipe with her as a souvenir of her happy childhood in Vienna. Around 1920, a specialist in puff pastry transformed it into the croissant we find today, now popular worldwide. A Parisian breakfast would not be complete without a croissant, whether it is in a half-moon shape (in French it even once bore the poetic name of "bread of the moon") or elongated. Its light, crumbly, buttery pastry makes it an ode to simplicity and elegance.

Puff pastry has been in existence in Europe since the Middle Ages. The Crusaders brought back from afar recipes and new techniques that considerably widened the range of European sweet treats. The newly created guild of bakers improved the puff pastry that had come from the Middle East.

COJEAN

The Cojean restaurants are the stars of the new Parisian fast food scene—to eat in or to go. Since 2001, in their chic, sober restaurants—so chic that an episode of *Sex and the City* was filmed in this restaurant, near Pont Neuf (facing page), seasonal cakes (lemon, ginger, carrot, and chocolate), and small Portuguese custard cakes, *pasteis de nata* (above center) are on offer.

BLÉ SUCRÉ

It's never easy to find really good madeleines: these are truly soft and melt-in-the-mouth, thanks to the high-quality butter from the Charente region (pages 134–135).

Its airy lightness is a result of the work of Guillaume Tirel, master pastry chef to kings Charles V and then Charles VI of France; Tirel was nicknamed Taillevent (wind-slicer) because his pastry was so light it seemed to be sliced from the wind. Puff pastry is one of the most difficult forms of pastry to make, and it can make or break the reputation of a pastry chef. The preparation of puff pastry is a major art in pastry making, not unrelated to mathematics or architecture. It requires absolute precision, the finest ingredients, and exemplary skills. Until the seventeenth century, puff-pastry pies with fruit were served only as part of the meal. When tea, coffee, and chocolate—all wildly popular at the courts—began arriving from the New World, they required some sort of solid food accompaniment, and traditional fruit pies using puff pastry had to be adapted.

A virtuoso puff pastry chef—nothing less is required for superlative results—had the idea of reducing the size of the circle of puff pastry used for pies, garnishing it with applesauce or cooked pieces of apple, and folding it over. The apple turnover was born. This is how the *Pastissier françois* (The French Pastry Chef), a recipe book dating from the seventeenth century, describes the *chausson aux pommes*: a chubby-cheeked, neatly trimmed pastry filled with a compote made of apples that have spent the night soaking in a vanilla syrup before being gently simmered. Stohrer still makes them this way, and if you arrive just as they are removed from the oven and are lucky enough to eat one warm, the pleasure will be a revelation. Even better is the *chausson* filled not with stewed apples but with a whole, fresh apple. The true flavor of the fruit is thus contained in the pastry. There are few bakers and pastry chefs who make it; one is Christophe Vasseur, whose lovely bakery is near to the Canal Saint Martin in the tenth arrondissement in Paris. The *chausson aux pommes* is suitable for eating at any time of the day, morning or afternoon, if you are feeling a little peckish, desperately need something sweet, or are overcome with a craving for an epicurean moment.

DES GÂTEAUX ET DU PAIN
Claire Damon's boutique, both pastry shop and bakery, is a surprising place. Look through the deceptively simple shop window (below right) and you will never guess what temptations await you through the doorway. First comes the long counter of *viennoiseries* (pages 138–139) and then, in the back, set off by shimmering satin drapes, you will see the cakes. It is perhaps their range of loaf cakes that is the most impressive and original (facing page): the spice bread, the lemon loaf, the giuanduja loaf, redcurrant and violet, caramel with salty butter, and more.

Another classic made of puff pastry is the *pain au chocolat*, or chocolate roll. In 1847, the Fry's chocolate company in Bristol, England first succeeded in molding chocolate into a bar. In France, Menier industrialized the production of chocolate bars. Bringing together chocolate bars and puff pastry seemed the obvious thing to do. Puff pastry, previously shaped into half-circles, was now folded into plump rectangles to contain the long, slim stick of chocolate slipped into the middle. The creation blends sweetness and an airy texture with crunchiness; the smoothness of butter is countered by the bitterness of chocolate, giving rise to a surprising balance. This *viennoiserie* pastry flakes away in the hand and is a pleasure to bite into. It is particularly good to eat at around ten or eleven o'clock in the morning; children will enjoy it in the afternoon after school. Anyone who is curious or blasé, who likes change but still wants to maintain certain traditions, should try the pains au chocolat with two sticks of chocolate, or even those with chocolate chips.

Although the *palmier*, or palm-leaf pastry (sometimes known as pig ears or elephant ears in English) is not one of the more popular children's snacks in France, *palmier* fans will go from shop to shop to compare its delicacy, crunchiness, and more or less caramelized taste. The *palmier* takes its name from its shape: it resembles the leaves of the tree that evokes blue skies and hot sun. Its puff pastry is generously sprinkled with sugar, rolled over, and sliced before it is baked. It is in the oven that it obtains its characteristic crisp texture and caramelized crunch. It is never better than when the pastry is made with premium flour and butter; the skill of the baker's hand is another prerequisite for its lightness.

But the pinnacle of puff pastry creation is the *galette des rois*, the kings' cake. It is eaten once a year to celebrate Twelfth Night, when the Three Kings visited baby Jesus. There is a traditional game that it would be sacrilege not to play before eating the cake: the youngest child in attendance is asked to sit under the table, from where he or she designates the recipient of each slice as it is cut. There is a lucky charm hidden in the filling, and so the child indirectly decides who will be the winner. Whoever finds the charm wears a golden paper crown (courtesy of the pastry shop) and can choose a king or queen to wear the second crown (also provided by the pastry shop). French children are torn between which they like best: eating the warm, golden pastry that gives off its mild buttery fragrance, that flakes between their fingers, and whose almond cream melts in their mouths? Or is it more fun to be designated king or queen of the evening? This seemingly simple cake is surprisingly difficult to make; very few pastry shops sell outstanding *galettes*. A good *galette des rois* must be the color of amber: too pale a shade betrays underbaked puff pastry that will probably be too heavy. The traditional garnish of a

DU PAIN ET DES IDÉES
In this old-fashioned bakery
near the Canal Saint Martin in
the tenth arrondissement,
you will find the Mouna, a
traditional North African
brioche-type recipe, also
found in Provence, that is
delightfully flavored with
orange-blossom water.
Choose between the plain
Mouna or the loaf scattered
with sugar.

DU PAIN ET DES IDÉES
Not only is this one of the
loveliest old-fashioned
bakeries in Paris, it is also
one of the best. Its counters
and large pottery dishes piled
up with specialties are refilled
several times a day, and are
always empty by day's end,
thanks to the many fans who
flock to it (above center and
facing page). From its apple
turnover filled with a whole
fresh apple (above left), to its
pistachio rolls (above right)
and its *pains au chocolat*
(pages 144–145), all are
baked with the highest
quality butter, making the
choice extremely difficult.

galette is the almond cream (a mixture of butter and ground blanched almonds) or the frangipane (a pastry cream mixed with the almond cream). Bakers and pastry chefs who choose to follow the authentic tradition either prepare a "dry" *galette* (without garnish) or one with a filling. The filling between the two layers of puff pastry requires a precise dose of each ingredient: the combination of its velvety texture with the fragile puff pastry is a work of art that not all pastry chefs master. Throughout January, *galette* lovers discuss the tastes and flavors of their favorites, but all agree that the major criterion of success is a creamy, light frangipane that is neither too sweet nor too fatty. In the south of France, Epiphany is celebrated not with a puff pastry *galette* but with a round brioche with candied fruits. In Paris, some pastry chefs prepare this cake, offering a choice between puff pastry and brioche pastry.

The yeast pastry brioche is a grand classic of *viennoiserie*. In his *Encyclopédie*, Diderot called it a "*magnificence onéreuse.*" This magnificence is said to be from Normandy, no doubt because of the butter that gives the yeast dough its inimitable flavor and texture. The cute little head of the Parisian brioche can be devoured in a mouthful; the rest—the body—can be broken off with the fingers, liberating the fragrances of flour, egg, and yeast from the fluffy pastry. In the seventeenth century, the Parisian pastry shop most famous for its brioches was the Flechner boutique. It stood at the corner of Rue Saint-Antoine and Rue Saint-Paul, near Bastille. The ingredients that make up the dough cannot be changed: flour, eggs, milk, and butter—unchanged since its creation—and, of course, yeast. To make it, however, is a delicate process involving timeless knowledge and skill so that the yeast forms the right-sized alveoli in order to give the brioche both its fine texture and its strength. The dough rises—"swells" might be more appropriate to describe the process—for several hours in a deep, fluted mold in a warm place free of drafts. The least little breeze might cool the dough, destroying the work accomplished by the yeast. When the dough begins to overflow the sides of the mold, the baker

bastes it with egg yolk and puts it in the oven. Mouthwatering, warm smells begin to radiate from the delicately tasty brioche. The brioche is usually made plain—it is best this way—or else with coarse grains of sugar sprinkled on top. Brioches are either small or in a larger size for sharing; in this category is the richer brioche mousseline, or chiffon brioche, which is recognizable from its high cylinder shape, whose name is suggestive of its almost ethereal quality. Marie-Antoinette's infamous comment, made when the hungry masses were calling for bread, which is usually translated into English as "Let them eat cake," referred to brioche; at the time brioche was more like a loaf of bread than the butter- and egg-rich, almost cake-like loaves made today. Its mild sweetness enhances the flavor of spreads with more pronounced sweetness such as preserves, honey, and chocolate.

Brioche dough can be attractively rolled into a snail shape to enclose a pastry cream generously sprinkled with rum-soaked raisins: a delicious *pain aux raisins*, or raisin roll. When it is baked, the entire pastry caramelizes, creating a particularly luscious, eminently edible cake. Sometimes rum is replaced by cinnamon, a special treat for lovers of this warm, vibrantly sensual spice.

Having done the rounds of French *viennoiseries*, it is clear that they are vulnerable to the caprices of the weather, cannot be kept waiting, and are a great way to start the day. In pastry shops, *viennoiseries* are set out next to a variety of other treats to go that travel well. These, unlike the pastries with a short shelf life described above, have been deliberately designed to keep longer—they contain no cream. They meet the same criteria for excellence, and it is worth tasting both those made by the great pastry chefs using traditional recipes and those made by innovators keen to experiment with new flavors. Among smaller variety—most people cannot resist eating more than one—are the *financiers* and the madeleines.

The most famous of these small cakes, the madeleine, described in Marcel Proust's *Swann's Way* as "the little scallop-shell of pastry, so richly sensual under its severe, religious folds" is a truly wonderful invention, that Proust used as a no less wonderful time machine, by way of which he was transported back to times past. It is often believed to have originated in Normandy because the writer enjoyed it there, but in fact it is from Commercy, a town in the eastern French region of Lorraine. The legend goes that it had royal origins. Once upon a time, there was a dethroned king, Stanislas Leczinski, who came to live in France. Today he would be known as someone with a sweet tooth, and he loved to provide delectable sweets for his guests. One day, disaster struck. His cook walked off the job without even preparing dessert. A servant did her best to make up for it by making cakes small

AOKI
The *panettone*, a type of sweet bread from Italy, is prepared as a small individual cake (and filled with raisins). Lightly dusted with sugar, its dry crust belies the soft, tender interior (facing page).

SÉBASTIEN DÉGARDIN
For fans of puff pastry, it is at its best in the *palmier*. Well-caramelized leaf edges add the merest hint of bitterness to the crisp cookie (below left).

BLÉ SUCRÉ
And here is yet more caramel, this time on the golden crust of a simple custard flan, where it contrasts neatly with the firm yet creamy custard (below right).

LADURÉE

For many pastry fans, Ladurée is synonymous with macaroons. The sheer delight of their rose or orange-blossom macaroons is quite unforgettable. However, in the exquisite surroundings of their patisserie on the Champs Elysées (pages 148–149), you will first be taken by their plump, golden *viennoiseries*, and then by their cream cakes, before you reach the almost infinite choice of flavored macaroons.

CUPCAKES & CO

A cute, all-pink boutique just made of all things nice (above center). Cupcakes have arrived in France. Creamy or pastel-colored icings (above left and right) are a delicious topping to these toy-sized cakes that already have established classics, like carrot cake and red velvet (facing page).

enough to hold in her hand. The recipe had come down to her from her grandmother, and she baked them in the scallop shells so plentiful in the region because Commercy was on El Camino de Santiago, the pilgrims' route on Saint James's Way. Stanislas was delighted with these pretty, soft biscuits, mildly flavored with lemon and butter. His guests enjoyed them just as much. To thank the servant, Madeleine, who had made them, he gallantly named them—or so goes the legend—after her.

Madeleines are not the only treat for which we have to thank the king. Exile sent him wandering through Europe, picking up the kugelhopf, a cake known since the late Middle Ages in Germany and the Eastern European countries. Some years later, Marie-Antoinette, apparently just as much a gourmande—and, as we have seen, already responsible for importing the croissant—brought the recipe with her. She could not imagine taking her breakfast without the kugelhopf that she had so enjoyed during her Vienna childhood. At about this time, the region of Alsace adopted the cake, and it became the traditional cake for weddings and christenings there. In 1840, a pastry chef named Georges from Strasbourg opened a boutique in Paris, in the Chaussée d'Antin neighborhood, and displayed the delicious yeast-raised dough, so similar to the brioche, with a generous scattering of raisins. The kugelhopf was an immediate success—and no wonder, for it is as tasty as it is attractive. It is baked in a mold similar to that used for the savarin, but the sides are higher and fluted with decorative swirls. The buttered mold is scattered with thinly sliced almonds that create a decorative pattern on the fluting. Once it has baked and is cooled, the kugelhopf is dusted with a cloud of confectioners' sugar. Although the recipe has remained unchanged to this day, few Parisian pastry chefs have it on sale. To find one of the very best, you must make your way to near the Bois de Vincennes, east of the city, to Stéphane Vandermeersch's pastry shop. His light, airy version is available on weekends only. The thin crust exudes a delicious smell of butter, and there is only one new twist to the tradition: the hazelnuts replacing the almonds on the crown.

Even though kugelhopf is not very well known these days, it is highly recommended for leisurely Sunday teas, in the same way as what the French call "cakes" are. What the French call a "cake" is what is known to the English-speaking world as a fruitcake, originally from Scotland. A raised dough with generous helpings of raisins and rum-soaked, candied fruits make up the basic recipe. When the cake is removed from the oven and has been allowed to cool, it is topped with sliced almonds and bright red glacéed cherries.

This cheerfully colored, multiflavored cake was invented by a pastry chef by the name of Michel who took his inspiration from the Dundee Cake, a dense, rich, buttery fruit cake whose most significant ingredients are candied orange peel and blanched almonds. The discovery that changed the cake-making world, in the midst of an era of industrial discoveries, was a chemical raising agent. This recent invention brought a touch of magic into pastry making, and of course considerably lightened the dough of the fruitcake. Monsieur Michel owned a tearoom, and Parisians thronged there to taste this new cake whose slices made a wonderful display of brightly colored, cheery fruits. And not only was it attractive, it was also mouthwatering. For added chic, the English word "cake" was used, and M. Michel's creation became the new "must-have" cake. So much so, in fact, that Félix Potain, a grocer who had already opened one of the first chains of stores in Paris, included the trendy cake in his range of products. The best Parisian pastry makers have created some quite astonishing variations on the theme: at the Plaza Athénée hotel, Christophe Michalak has come up with an amusing series. The *toasté* is sold in a pretty long metal box, round and red. Very film-starry. The plain loaf is encased in another chocolate one, creating a subtle harmony that is the hallmark of this iconoclastic, talented chef. They are baked fresh daily, one for every taste: chocolate or lemon for the traditionalists among us, and carrot or ginger for the more daring.

VANDERMEERSCH
In January, the *galette des rois*, one of the best in Paris, takes pride of place in this old boutique. The weekend kugelhopf is just as outstanding.

BISTROT PAUL BERT
This bistro offers mini *cannelés*, a Bordeaux specialty, with coffee. Like all good *cannelés*, they are dark and crisp on the outside, and almost white and soft inside (page 154).

BLÉ SUCRÉ
One of the draws of puff pastry *viennoiseries* is its caramelized aspect, as seen on the edges of these delicious apple turnovers here (page 155).

Another teatime classic in Paris is the *quatre quarts*, literally "four fourths," a close relative of the pound cake. It is not commonly found in Parisian bakeries and pastry shops, perhaps because it has maintained its reputation as a "domestic cake," as the Larousse dictionary defined it in 1893. With its four basic ingredients, each weighing the same, it is quick and easy to make at home. Simply combine the flour, eggs, sugar, and butter, and then add something else to jazz it up if you want. Children love this cake for their afternoon snack, especially when it is made with chocolate. Today's pastry chefs make *quatre quarts* with raspberries or pistachios.

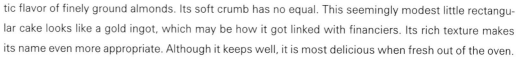

Yet another small cake of the same variety—the best for eating on the go—is the *financier*, with its characteristic flavor of finely ground almonds. Its soft crumb has no equal. This seemingly modest little rectangular cake looks like a gold ingot, which may be how it got linked with financiers. Its rich texture makes its name even more appropriate. Although it keeps well, it is most delicious when fresh out of the oven.

Yet another cake that makes good use of almonds—it uses almond paste—is the somewhat forgotten *pain de Gênes*, or "Genoa bread," which saw the light of day in 1855, thanks to Fauvel, a pastry chef at Frascati's in Paris, who replaced flour with ground almonds. It was a belated but still relevant homage to General Massena's soldiers, who—during the Italian Campaign—survived thanks to the stocks of almonds amassed by the Genovese when the city was besieged by the Austrians in 1800.

From Genoa we also have the genoise, used as a base for many filled cakes, such as the *fraisier* (a popular strawberry cake), but which is also good when served plain. Whole eggs beaten with sugar are the starting point for this recipe. In the United States, families often have secret recipes for sponge cakes that are transmitted from generation to generation and which are used to prepare little cakes finished with various toppings—from butter cream to chocolate ganache—known as "cupcakes", or "fairy cakes" in England. A long-time favorite among children in all English-speaking countries, they are making an appearance in Paris. Meanwhile chocolate chip cookies, developed in the United States in the 1930s, have been eaten in Paris for many years: even Pierre Hermé has his own version. Another American invention, brownies, now have a place in just about all Paris bakeries, and some of the best Parisian pastry chefs have developed their own recipes. That venerable Parisian institution, Berthillon, is among those that serve them.

All these cakes are made to be eaten on the go, and are the perfect solution for Parisians who seem to have less and less time to sit down at the table for an elaborate cake, but who still can't resist a scrumptious sweet treat.

JEAN-PAUL HÉVIN
The cheesecake, a cake that originated in Central Europe and made its way to North America, is also much appreciated in France. In some regions in this country, it is even a traditional cake. This one is exceptionally deep and light. It does not matter if you give in to temptation: it is prepared with skim milk cream cheese. Jean-Paul Hévin calls it his Mazaltov, and its whiteness stands out in the window filled with chocolate cakes.

BERTHILLON
Sumptuous vanilla-flavored chantilly sprinkled with caramel and hazelnut praline shards is a perfect accompaniment for any number of cakes (page 160).

Our Favorite Addresses

Where should you go for the best chocolate cakes, the widest range of fruit tarts, the most scrumptious éclairs, and the most delicate macaroons? Who should be your trusted supplier of a *galette des rois* in January, a summery strawberry *fraisier*, or your breakfast *viennoiseries*? Here, we have listed the best patisseries in Paris and the pick of the *salons de thé*. This address book is not a catalog of their pastries. We wanted to share with you what we loved best when we tasted their specialties. Pastry chefs have their own classics that they revisit in their own inimitable styles; they create seasonal collections, and follow their whims. You will not necessarily, therefore, find exactly the cake that enchanted us so much. Taste a new one, for Parisian patisserie is a constantly renewed and evolving art. Keep in mind that closing days are not always those you might expect. Some also close in summer; check the website or call ahead.

The page numbers in this list of addresses refer to the photos; take a look before you visit.

ANGELINA
Salons de thé
226, Rue de Rivoli, 75001
Tel.: +33 1 42.60.82.00
2, Place de la Porte Maillot (Palais des Congrès), 75017
Tel.: +33 1 40.68.22.50
You will find the flagship of this *salon de thé*, renowned for its 1900s decor, beneath the vaulted arches of the Rue de Rivoli, opposite the Tuileries Gardens. To sample the house specialties, there's a good chance that you will have to stand in line for a while. Try the famous Mont Blanc or vanilla mille-feuilles as a snack with their remarkable hot chocolate or a dessert after a light lunch. Every morning, at 11 a.m., between 400 and 1,000 Mont Blancs are prepared for all Angelina's *salons de thé*. According to the pastry chef, Sébastien Bauer, this is the right time to try one, for that is when the texture is perfect. You will also find Angelina's Mont Blancs and mille-feuilles at Lipp, the famous brasserie. The Eva tartlet, with chocolate and raspberries, was an instant hit with the actress Eva Longoria, and has recently been added to the list of favorite confections here.
Open daily.
See photos pp. 50–51.

AOKI
35, Rue de Vaugirard, 75006
Tel.: +33 1 45.44.48.90
56, Boulevard de Port-Royal, 75005
Tel.: +33 1 45.35.36.80
There are also three boutiques in Tokyo.
3-4-1 Shinkokusai BLD
Marunouchi,chiyoda-ku Tokyo
Tel.: +81 3 5293 2800
www.sadaharuaoki.com
Near the Luxembourg Gardens, Japanese pastry chef Aoki's boutique gives pride of place to lemon, strawberry, and matcha tea cakes, all of whose bright colors will draw you irresistibly to them. His *financiers* are delicious, as are the chocolate and lemon loaf cakes, and the traditional Italian panettone. The salted caramel tarts won our unanimous approval when we did our tastings. Chocolate lovers will find happiness with the molten chocolate cake and the Black Forest gâteau. There are over fifteen flavors of macaroons, as stunningly attractive as they are delicious. Our personal favorites are peach, violet, and yuzu.
Closed Monday and public holidays.
See photos pp. 10–11, 72–73, 122, 123, 124–125, 146

L'ARPÈGE
84, Rue de Varenne, 75007
Tel.: +33 1 47.05.09.06
www.alain-passard.com
In this three-Michelin-starred restaurant, taste the exquisite apple tart, the Bouquet of Roses. The apples are sculpted like blossoms and laid out on a crisp pastry. If you want to impress your guests, you can order it a day ahead and fetch it at the restaurant.
Closed Saturday and Sunday.
See photo p. 16

BERKO
23, Rue Rambuteau, 75004
Tel.: +33 1 40.29.02.44
Close to the Georges Pompidou museum, a pastry chef with a passion for the United States and its cheesecakes, crumbles, and pecan pies, ventured to introduce cupcakes to the French. They were an immediate success, and Berko soon created an entire range comprising some twenty flavors, which vary with the seasons. The best-seller is salted butter caramel. You will also find mini cookies in bite sizes. Try the chocolate, calisson from Aix-en-Provence, bilberry, speculoos, cherry, rose, Nutella, and more.
Closed Monday.

BERTHILLON
Salon de thé
29–31, Rue Saint Louis en l'île, 75004
Tel.: +33 1 43.54.31.61
Berthillon's ice creams are renowned the world over. Parisians and tourists agree that this ice-cream maker is the best in Paris. For three generations, Berthillon has been churning ice creams using only the very finest ingredients. The *salon de thé* and its pastries have not yet acquired the same fame, but this is no reason not to go in to taste Monsieur Berthillon's granddaughter Muriel's cakes. She does a sumptuous tarte Tatin with a generous helping of apples, and a *tarte fine* with caramelized apples. Unless of course, you'd rather taste the brownies—not to be missed when accompanied by the quite fantastic chantilly cream they make here. There is no doubt: with its delicate Madagascar vanilla flavor, it is the best we have tasted.

Closed Monday and Tuesday.
See photos pp. 6, 54–55, 86–87, 160

BISTROT PAUL BERT
18, Rue Paul Bert, 75011
Tel.: +33 1 43.72.24.01
This is neither a pastry shop nor a *salon de thé*, but an old-style bistro not far from the Faubourg St-Antoine in the eleventh arrondissement. Loyal clients claim it serves one of the very best Paris-Brest cakes in Paris. François Simon, a food critic, shares this opinion. In his blog he says of the Paul Bert bistro, "The Paris-Brest I ate there was perfectly made, with exactly the right degree of crispness." Their strawberry and raspberry macaroons, served with fresh fruit, are equally good.
Closed Sunday and Monday.
See photos pp. 20, 21, 154

BLÉ SUCRÉ
7, Rue Antoine Vollon, 75012
Tel.: +33 1 43.40.77.73
Just a few minutes' walk from the Aligre market, you will find the best *viennoiseries* imaginable, not to mention outstanding *financiers* and madeleines. The heart-shaped tarte Tatin is simply divine. The chocolate Vollon, the house classic, is a dark chocolate zabaglione over an almond *dacquoise* pastry base. According to Christophe Michalak, pastry chef at the luxury Plaza Athénée hotel, the best mille-feuilles in Paris are to be found at the Blé Sucré. When the weather is sunny, three tables are brought out for you to savor your delectables opposite the pretty bandstand of the Square Trousseau.

Closed Sunday afternoon and all Monday.
See photos pp. 40, 41, 128, 134–135, 155, 157

LE BOULANGER DE MONGE

123, Rue Monge, 75005
Tel.: +33 1 43.37.54.20
www.leboulangerdemonge.com
At a busy corner on Rue Monge, the incessant coming and going of clients is a clear indicator that what is sold here is the best. The *viennoiseries* are simply outstanding, the brioche, with its enticing smell of yeast, is light and fluffy, and the puff pastry of the *pain au chocolat* is as crisp as you could wish for. There is also a wide range of fruit tarts, such as redcurrant, rhubarb, pear with brown sugar, and more.
Closed Monday.

CARETTE

Salon de thé
4, Place du Trocadéro, 75016
Tel.: +33 1 47.27.98.85
www.carette-paris.com
If you're a morning person, a good place to come for coffee and delicious *viennoiseries* is Carette, open from 7 a.m. Sit outside and enjoy the view of the Eiffel Tower. Should you rise later, it is open non-stop, until 12.30 a.m. during the week and 11.30 p.m. over the weekend. Enjoy one of the house specialties: choose from the traditional Saint Honoré or the Paris-Carette, a revisited Paris-Brest with vanilla macaroon, pistachio cream, and fresh raspberries. Should you wish to spoil a special person who's a fan of both chocolate and macaroons, you can order a large chocolate macaroon for four to ten people.
Open every day.
See photos pp. 34–35, 64–65

COJEAN

3, Place du Louvre, 75001
Tel.: +33 1 40.13.06.80
Many branches—see their Internet site for information: www.cojean.fr.
Don't be surprised by the number of American tourists you see: an episode of *Sex and the City* was filmed here. This branch is ideally located in the center of Paris, opposite the Louvre and the lovely church of Saint Germain de l'Auxerrois. The *salon de thé* serves healthy light food to eat in or to go. The restaurant is beautifully decorated with its original woodwork and is extremely popular. Everything is prepared daily and no client can resist the desserts. The Cojean company already has some fifteen locations. Not only do they sell delicious Portuguese flans, the small *pasteis de nata*, they also offer a wide choice of delicious cakes. The best-sellers are the chocolate cake and the carrot cake. Our particular favorite is the ginger cake.
Closed Sunday.
See photos pp. 132, 133

PHILIPPE CONTICINI

La Pâtisserie des Rêves
93, Rue du Bac, 75007
Tel. : + 33 1 42.84.00.82
As this book goes to press, the boutique of this renowned pastry chef is about to open. Close to the Bon Marché department store, you will be able to enjoy the return of the great classics with a contemporary take: tarte Tatin, coffee mocha, Paris-Brest, and mille-feuilles (the mille-feuilles will be served on Sunday only).
Closed Sunday afternoon and Monday.

CHRISTIAN CONSTANT

37, Rue d'Assas, 75007
Tel.: +33 1 53.63.15.15
Just a short walk away from the Luxembourg Gardens, a dark chocolate symphony is practically audible. All true chocolate lovers already know the chocolate tart for which the boutique is so famous. This great chocolate maker showcases his talents in over a dozen creations. Depending on the cake, you will find chocolate with jasmine-flavored green tea, lemon, cinnamon, and raspberry. For anyone who's not too fond of chocolate, there is the Pont Royal, a light hazelnut dessert.
Open every day.

DALLOYAU

101, Rue du Faubourg Saint-Honoré, 75008
Tel.: +33 1 42.99.90.00
5, Boulevard Beaumarchais, 75004
Tel.: +33 1 48.87.89.88
Many boutiques in Paris. Consult the website: www.dalloyau.fr.
There are also boutiques in Toyko, Seoul, and Kuwait.
Near the Elysée Palace, the official residence of the French President, on the ultra chic Faubourg Saint-Honoré, this venerable establishment has provided delicious treats to gourmets for several generations now. All the traditional desserts are there, and Dalloyau specializes in large-size cakes. All its boutiques offer the *religieuses*—chocolate or coffee—for six, as well as macaroons with seasonal flavors (caramel apple, raspberry, and so on) for six. Chocolate lovers, who all know the famous Opéra with its hint of coffee, will also like the Faubourg, which brings together chocolate and vanilla.
Open every day.

SEBASTIEN DÉGARDIN

29, Boulevard de Reuilly, 75012
Tel.: +33 1 43.07.77.59
Near the impressive Lion Fountain on the Place Daumesnil, you will find an outstanding pastry maker who was pastry chef at the world-renowned Troisgros restaurant in Roanne. He delights food-lovers with his high-quality creations, including the *polonaise*, made by very few chefs, the chestnut Mont Blanc, and the strawberry *fraisier*, just as light as the passion fruit *passiflore*. Don't miss the hazelnut éclairs, the perfect apricot tart, and the Genoa bread, a rare cake with a soft crumb.
Closed Monday.
See photos pp. 38, 39, 127, 147

ARNAUD DELMONTEL

(1) 39, Rue des Martyrs, 75009
Tel.: +33 1 48.78.29.33
(2) 57 Rue Damrémont, 75017
Tel.: +33 1 42.64.59.63
www.arnaud-delmontel.com
When you are on Rue des Martyrs with the Sacré-Cœur in sight, don't miss one of Paris's best bakeries. It is also an excellent patisserie, famous for its loaf cakes and Viennoiseries. Taste the pistachio mille-feuilles and the lemon and orange tart. Jean-François Piège, former head chef at the Crillon, enthuses over the salted butter caramel *galette*, whose puff pastry is memorable.
(1) Closed Tuesday. (2) Closed Sunday afternoon and Monday.

LES DEUX ABEILLES

Salon de thé
189, Rue de l'Université, 75007
Tel.: +33 1 45.55.64.04
A stone's throw away from the Quai Branly Museum, this old-style *salon de thé* may well remind customers of their grandmothers' dining rooms, and the cakes of those their grandmothers used to make, in the days when baking was undertaken with heartfelt enthusiasm. This is an address known only to its fans, who like to get together for lunch there. The lunch always ends with a dessert, for the dessert trolley is quite irresistible. Their cheesecake, molten chocolate cake, chocolate almond cake, berry crumble, and spice tart are served warm. All the cakes, including the lemon meringue pie, a sheer delight, can be ordered to take away.
Closed Sunday.
See photos pp. 29, 156

LAURENT DUCHÊNE

2, Rue Wurtz, 75013
Tel.: +33 1 45.65.00.77
www.laurent-duchene.com
If you're not familiar with the charming neighborhood of La Butte aux Cailles, you'll have to hunt a little. Once you know the place, you'll go there on auto-pilot. The cakes, made by the chef who was named Best Craftsman in France in 1993, are strikingly audacious, with ingredients like coriander, chocolate, and lime. Laurent Duchêne makes an outstanding molten chocolate cake and a rhubarb-raspberry tart. For coffee lovers, there is an all-coffee pastry that brings together a variety of textures—soft cake, cream, and mousse—using a single flavor. The house motto on the shop window promises you "Gourmandise, emotion, flavors, and temptations," and it's a promise that is kept.
Closed Sunday.
See photos pp. 2, 82–85, 118–121

Our Favorite Addresses

FAUCHON
Salons de thé
(1) Le café: 30, Place de la Madeleine, 75008
(2) La boulangerie: 24/26, Place de la Madeleine, 75008
Tel.: +33 1 70.39.38.00
Stores worldwide; see website.
LONDON:
Selfridges
400 Oxford Street, London W1A 1AB
NEW YORK:
Food Emporium (Bridge Market Store)
405 East 59th Street, NY 10022
www.fauchon.fr
Behind the Madeleine Church, just above the pastry shop, Le Café offers you the latest in contemporarily designed cakes, in harmony with the flashy pink and silver decor by Christian Biecher. The éclairs are particularly spectacular and come in a range of pop-art designs. Flavors combine with fruits from the four corners of the earth. The chocolate-almond éclair, Madame Joconde, has icing Mona Lisa eyes that follow you, just like those of the real painting. *Wallpaper* magazine chose it as Best Teatime Treat 2009. These pastries can be enjoyed until 11 p.m. At La Boulangerie you'll find madeleines in all the flavors you could wish for—chocolate, caramel, dulce de leche, honey-pistachio, and more—displayed on a bench, in a nod to the church nearby.
(1) Open every day. (2) Closed Sunday.
See photos pp. 32, 33, 96, 97

DES GÂTEAUX ET DU PAIN
63, Boulevard Pasteur, 75015
Tel.: +33 1 45.38.94.29
Yann Pennors' contemporary decor is strikingly innovative: the cakes are not displayed in the shop window.

However, as soon as you enter, the delicious smell of butter will waft up from a huge table covered with *viennoiseries*. But where are the cakes so highly acclaimed by the great chefs? You'll find them at the back on the left, in a display case highlighted by shimmering drapes. There is a plump Saint Honoré, delicately flavored with orange blossom and milk chocolate, or violet-strawberry-blackberry topped with spicy caramel chantilly cream. The flavors change with the seasons. Their *religieuse* with salted caramel, the lemon-candied lemon tart, and the pear tart with Mauritius cane sugar are justifiably famous. An important piece of advice if you like to sleep in: the mille-feuilles are made on weekends only, and by noon, they are all sold out!
Closed Tuesday.
See photos pp. 15, 25, 110–111, 115, 136–139

LA GRANDE EPICERIE DU BON MARCHE
26–38, Rue de Sèvres, 75007
Tel.: +33 1 44.39.81.00
www.lagrandeepicerie.fr
This food hall is extremely popular with gourmets, who appreciate the fine range of products on offer. The patisserie is right at the entrance, impossible to miss. The Vertical mille-feuilles combines chocolate-nougatine puff pastry and vanilla cream. Le Gâteau is a graphically designed towering square alternating pistachio sponge, milk chocolate mousse, dark chocolate mousse, and raspberry jelly. It is sold in a chocolate box, in individual portions or for eight to ten people. We recommend the light, delicious Yuzu Mania, a pretty white pastry decorated with red calligraphic strokes—this is certainly the cake that won our hearts. It comprises a Genoa bread filled with yuzu cream and lime mousse. The Tonka is more classic, bringing together vanilla and chocolate—a sheer delight. The *viennoiseries* may be less spectacular but they are just as tempting and delicious.
Closed Sunday.
See photos pp. 28, 88–91, 108–109

PIERRE HERMÉ
72, Rue Bonaparte, 75006
Tel.: +33 1 43.54.47.77
and at:
(1) 185, Rue de Vaugirard, 75015
Tel.: +33 1 47.83.89.96
(2) 4, Rue Cambon, 75001
Tel.: +33 1 58.62.43.17
(Macaroons and chocolates only)
133, Avenue des Champs-Elysées, drugstore Publicis, 75008
Tel.: +33 1 43.54.47.77
There are also seven branches in Tokyo, including one at:
The New Otani – 4-1 Kioi-cho, Chiyoda-ku, Tokyo 102-8578
Tel.: +81 (0)3 3221 7252
www.pierreherme.com
The holy grail of French patisseries is located close by the Place Saint-Sulpice. With a perpetual line snaking out on to the sidewalk, you will have to wait for the Infiniment Vanille or the coffee tart, the praline 2000 feuilles, and the star, Ispahan, a macaroon with rose, litchis, and fresh raspberries. Works of chocolate art, such as the Carrément Chocolat, the perfect square for bitter-chocolate lovers, and Plénitude, a subtle combination of chocolate and caramel textures and flavors, will delight you. The boutique on the Rue Vaugirard, not far from the Montparnasse Railway Station, is quieter and more easily accessible. The boutique on Rue Cambon near the Tuileries Gardens is dedicated to macaroons and chocolates. A veritable monument to macaroons, it offers a range from the great classics to the most audacious: chocolate-caramel, wasabi-grapefruit, passion fruit-milk chocolate, chestnut-green matcha tea, white truffle-hazelnut, rose, salted caramel, and more.
Open every day. (1) Closed Monday. (2) Closed Sunday.
See photos pp. 6, 24, 66–69, 98–103

JACQUES GENIN
Salon de thé
133, Rue de Turenne, 75003
Tél.: +33 1 45.77.29.01
In the heart of the Marais district, this recently opened *salon de thé* is very different from the more classical or cozy Parisian *salons de thé*. Here, the decor is contemporary and sober. Jacques Genin, who calls himself a "fondeur en chocolat," a foundry worker in chocolate, is also a fine pastry chef. He will prepare one of a

large choice of mille-feuilles specially for you while you wait—praline, chocolate, caramel, and more—and you can also order them for eight people. His Paris-Brest, lime tarts, éclairs, and chocolate tart are just as delicious.
Closed Monday.

JEAN-PAUL HÉVIN
(1) 231, Rue Saint-Honoré, 75001
Salon de thé
Tel.: +33 1 55.35.35.96
and at:
3, Rue Vavin, 75006
Tel.: +33 1 43.54.09.85
23 bis, Avenue de la Motte-Piquet, 75007
Tel.: +33 1 45.51.77.48
Jean-Paul Hévin products are also sold through boutiques in Japan and Hong Kong.
www.jphevin.com
Near the Place Vendôme, famous for its jewelers, is a store that sells precious objects of another type: Jean-Paul Hévin's boutique specializes in chocolate. You can enjoy lunch upstairs in the *salon de thé*, finishing off with chocolate cakes like the Safi, chocolate mousse and bitter orange, and the Chocolat Framboise, chocolate mousse between a cacao sponge and a raspberry sponge. Only on Friday and Saturday will you be able to try the Mont Blanc, one of the best in Paris, and traditional cream puffs. Early in January, people line up for the chocolate *galette des rois* invented by Hévin. The chocolate macaroon is incredibly delicate—no less a chef than Pierre Hermé acclaims it highly. At the Saint-Honoré *salon de thé*, your chocolate tart will be served warm—it's an unforgettable experience!
Closed Sunday, Monday, and public holidays. (1) Closed Sunday and public holidays.
See photos pp. 48, 49, 58, 60–63, 158–159

LADURÉE
Salons de thé
75, Avenue des Champs-Elysées, 75008
Tel.: +331 40.75.08.75
and at:
16, Rue Royale, 75001
Tel.: +33 1 42.60.21.79
21, Rue Bonaparte, 75006
Tel.: +33 1 44.07.64.87

There are also branches in London, Monaco, Geneva, Lausanne, and Tokyo.

LONDON:

Harrods
87–135 Brompton Road, London.
SW1X 7XL
Tel.: +44 (0)203 155 0111
Burlington Arcade
71–72 Burlington Arcade, London.
W1J OQX
Tel.: +44 (0)207 491 9155
www.laduree.fr

The refined atmosphere that reigns in each Ladurée *salon de thé* is quite unique. The decor of the salon on Rue Royale, near Place de la Concorde, dates back to 1862. The salon on the Champs-Elysées was decorated by Jacques Garcia. Each one is a temple to the confectionery of macaroons, and the range is seemingly endless. There are the classics, always available: vanilla, coffee, raspberry, chocolate, bitter chocolate, rose petal, orange blossom, licorice, pistachio, blackcurrant, and violet, and more. In summer, you might find coconut, mint, and grenadine, and in winter, lemon, chestnut, and praline. In addition, there are the special, ephemeral creations; the one we like best is apple caramel. The cakes, too, are quite exquisite. The rose-raspberry Saint Honoré is delicious, as is the chocolate cake of the same name, and the mille-feuilles and simple raspberry tart are just as delectable. At the Champs-Elysées, you can choose from both savory and sweet dishes, from early morning (7.30 a.m.) to late at night (12.30 a.m.). The first Ladurée Bar has just opened. The boutique on the Champs-Elysées is open every day until 11 p.m. on weekdays, until 12.30 a.m. on Sunday morning, and on Sunday, until 10 pm.
See photos cover page, pp. 44–47, 105, 148, 149

ARNAUD LARHER

53, Rue Caulaincourt, 75018
Tel.: +33 1 42.57.68.08
www.arnaud-larher.com
In a romantic neighborhood of the eighteenth arrondissement, just off the Avenue Junot, Larher's shop window cannot be missed. This pastry chef was the Best Craftsman in France in 2007, and you will see

why before you even enter. Pierre Hermé speaks with great feeling of the art of the man who presides here, and Christophe Michalak simply adores his caramel Saint Honoré. Another star cake here is the chocolate and raspberry Monté Cristo, and there are mille-feuilles whose flavors change with the inspiration of the chef. One of the most popular cakes, the Toulouse-Lautrec, is ideal for chocolate lovers, and the panettones, too, are delicious.
Closed Sunday and Monday.

LECUREUIL

96, Rue de Lévis, 75017
Tel.: +33 1 42.27.28.27
www.lecureuil.fr
If you are food shopping at the many gourmet boutiques on Rue de Lévis, don't miss this delicious patisserie. You'll have to fight your way in to buy the glacéed chestnut *religieuse*, the mango and roasted pineapple tart, and the Bourdaloue pear tart.
Closed Sunday and Monday.

LENÔTRE

44, Rue d'Auteuil, 75016
Tel.: +33 1 45.24.52.52
10, Rue Saint Antoine, 75004
Tel.: +33 1 53.01.91.91
(1) 110, Avenue de France, 7013
Tel.: +33 1 44.97.01.39
Many branches; consult the website for the most convenient:
www.lenotre.fr
Boutiques also in Cannes and Nice and 35 branches in 12 countries worldwide.

LAS VEGAS:

Paris Las Vegas hotel
3645 Las Vegas Boulevard South, Las Vegas, Nevada PO. 3655
Tel.: +1 702 946 4341

Gaston Lenôtre had many loyal followers. They will remain faithful to him, continuing to enjoy his classics, like the Feuille d'Automne, a meringue and chocolate mousse, the Eléonore tart, puff pastry with apples, and the feathery light Schuss, with cream cheese and chantilly cream, not to mention the Succès, beloved of praline cream fans. Christophe Michalak, who knows what he's talking about, says that the best (two-stick) chocolate roll in Paris is on sale here.
Open every day. (1) Closed Saturday and Sunday.
See photos pp. 6, 30–31, 78, 79, 116, 117

LA MAISON DU CHOCOLAT

225, Rue du Faubourg Saint-Honoré, 75008
Tel.: +33 1 42.27.39.44
(1) 52, Rue François 1er, 75008
(*Salon de thé*)
Tel.: +33 1 47.23.38.25
(2) 8, Boulevard de la Madeleine, 75009
Tel.: +33 1 47.42.86.52
(3) Carrousel du Louvre
99, Rue de Rivoli, 75001
Tél.: +33 1 42.97.13.50
19, Rue de Sèvres, 75006
Tel.: +33 1 45.44.20.40
120, Avenue Victor Hugo, 75016
Tel.: +33 1 40.67.77.83
There are many branches of La Maison du Chocolat: consult the website to find the one most convenient for you:
www.lamaisonduchocolat.com
Boutiques also in Cannes, New York, London, Tokyo, and Hong Kong.

NEW YORK:

1018 Madison Avenue, New York 10075
30 Rockefeller Center, New York 10020
63 Wall Street, New York 10005

LONDON:

45–46 Piccadilly, London W1J ODS
Harrods
87–135 Brompton Road, London SW1X 7XL
www.lamaisonduchocolat.com
Obviously, this is *the* place for chocoholics to enjoy everything from the soft chocolate cake to the truffle mousse and the chocolate tart, not to mention the chocolate éclairs for which they are so well known. Perhaps the most surprising creations in this temple to chocolate

are the caramel pastries. The caramel éclairs jockey for pride of place with the chocolate éclairs and with the Rigoletto, which has a salted butter caramel ganache. In season, you'll find carefully selected French chestnuts made into a mousse in the unctuous Marroni tart. The Brésilien is a subtle combination of caramel, coffee mousse, and crunchy chocolate. On Sundays, keep in mind that the chocolate tart, éclairs, and the Rigoletto are not available. You will be able to make up for that with the creamy desserts.
Open every day except Sunday afternoon. (1) and (2) Closed Sunday. (3) Open every day.
See photos pp. 4–5, 74–77, 114

CARL MARLETTI

51, Rue Censier, 75005
Tel.: +33 1 43.31.68.12
www.carlmarletti.com
Just a short walk from the busy Rue Mouffetard, opposite the Saint-Médard church, is a pretty little boutique, all stone and marble, where you will find one of Paris's best lemon tarts. The pistachio éclairs and rose *religieuses* are as wonderful as the vanilla and chocolate-passion fruit mille-feuilles. Chocolate lovers will enjoy the Censier, available in different textures. The Caraïbe, with milk chocolate, passion fruit, and coconut, is the acme of refinement.
Closed Sunday afternoon and Monday.
See photos pp. 52, 53, 81

MILLET

103, Rue St Dominique, 75007
Tel.: +33 1 45.51.49.80
www.patisseriemillet.com
This neighborhood pastry shop makes classic cakes like the *polonaise, puits d'amour*, and the Mont Blanc. Eric Fréchon, a chef who has just been awarded his third Michelin star, is an ardent fan of their croissant, with its authentic buttery taste.
Open every day.

MULOT

(1) 76, Rue de Seine 75006
Tel.: +33 1 43.26.85.77
and at:
93, Rue Glacière, 75013
Tel.: +33 1 43.81.39.09

Our Favorite Addresses

6, Rue du Pas de la Mule, 75003
Tel.: +33 1 42.78.52.17
www.gerard-mulot.fr
Opposite the Saint-Germain market, halfway between the Saint-Sulpice Church and the Odéon Theater, don't miss Mulot's patisserie, an institution for the past twenty-five years. All the tarts are delicious, but the pear and grapefruit, and pear-almond, are superlative. A cake that is now hard to find is a clafoutis with Morello cherries, and another equally rare cake that can be ordered is the *polonaise*. The Amaryllis, a large macaroon with dried fruit and raspberries, rivals with the Coeur Frivole, which is made of two mousses, milk chocolate and dark chocolate. The meringues with chantilly cream are available on the weekend but must be specially ordered during the week.
Closed Monday. (1) Closed Wednesday.
See photos pp. 26, 27, 37, 70, 71, 106–107

PAIN DE SUCRE
14, Rue Rambuteau, 75003
Tel.: +33 1 45.74.68.92
www.patisseriepaindesucre.com
In the Marais quarter, just a few minutes' walk from the Pompidou Center, is a pocket-sized boutique with contemporary decor. Fruit is the predominant element in the pastries here. The tarts, with their layers of almond cream, have caramelized apples with rosemary, purple figs, and redcurrants. The pineapple éclair is simply divine. The Ephémère, with its meringue base with coconut and blackcurrants, and the Miss Marple—chestnut and quince—are extremely popular. The individual desserts in small glasses are the best in all Paris. You will not forget the unusual macaroon with chestnut honey and elderberry. The scones, and the raspberry and chocolate pound cakes are simply delicious.
Closed Tuesday and Wednesday.
See photos pp. 7, 13, 18, 19, 36, 80, 93, 94, 112, 113, 156

DU PAIN ET DES IDÉES
34, Rue Yves-Toudic, 75010
Tel.: +33 1 42.40.44.52
www.dupainetdesidees.com
There is a beautiful bakery near the Canal Saint Martin in the tenth arrondissement that is not to be missed, and not only for its 1889 decor, which has made it a listed building. The owner, Christophe Vasseur, used to work in fashion. He finally decided to learn to be a baker to make his childhood dream of baking bread come true. He succeeded, to the point of being named best baker in Paris in 2008 by the *Gault-Millau* guide. His bakery, which is full of clients from the moment it opens at 7 a.m., is the kingdom of *viennoiseries*. The traditional puff pastry, created using neither additives nor short cuts, is made from carefully selected premium ingredients. The butter, for example, is supplied by a small cooperative in Normandy. Du Pain et des Idées makes *viennoiseries* you

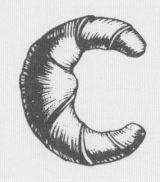

will not find elsewhere, such as a special version of an apple turnover, made not with apple sauce but with a half-apple baked with very little sugar in the puff pastry, giving you a taste of fruit as it was in turnovers of yesteryear. Another house specialty is the whirled croissant filled with unctuous pistachio pastry cream. There is also a good selection of seasonal fruit tarts.
Closed Saturday and Sunday.
See photos pp. 140–145

PLAZA ATHÉNÉE
25, Avenue Montaigne, 75008
Tel.: +33 1 53.67.66.00
www.plaza-athenee-paris.com
It is definitely worth going into the impressive Plaza Athénée Hotel and sitting down in the elegant Galerie des Gobelins to sample Christophe Michalak's pastries. Any gourmet worthy of the name simply has to try his cakes once in a lifetime. A word of advice: arrive before 3 p.m., for it is a popular place and fills up quickly. This way, you will have the choice of one of twenty desserts on the trolley: classics like the rum baba, the coffee éclair with its delicious hint of licorice, the mille-feuilles, and the chocolate, salted butter caramel, and redcurrant-violet *religieuses*. You will also be tempted by a selection of delicious loaf cakes.
Open daily.
See photos pp. 42, 43, 104

POÎLANE
(1) 8, Rue du Cherche-Midi, 75006
Tel.: +33 1 45.48.42.59
and at:
(2) 49, Boulevard de Grenelle, 75015
Tel.: +33 1 45.79.11.49
London:
46 Elizabeth Street, London SW1W 9PA
Tel.: +44 (0) 207 808 4910
www.poilane.fr
This world-renowned bakery makes fine *viennoiseries*. And in addition to their delicious cinnamon apple tarts and wonderful custard flans—some of the best in Paris—there is a cake not to be missed in January: the *galette des rois*. You can buy it either in its traditional version, with no filling in the delicate puff pastry, or with a hazelnut cream filling, one you will only find here.
(1 and 3) Closed Sunday. (2) Closed Monday.
See photos pp. 130, 131

PRALUS
35, Rue de Rambuteau, 75004
Tel.: +33 1 48.04.05.05
www.chocolats-pralus.com
The chocolate maker from the town of Roanne, who has set up shop in Paris, in the Marais district, makes one of the most delicious praline brioches in the city. It's called La Praluline, and it contains pink candied almonds and hazelnuts. The brioche is sent all over France and even farther, to customers in the USA and Japan. For chocolate fans who prefer theirs organic, there are chocolate slabs made from organic cacao. An important detail to keep in mind: during the week, the boutique is shut between 1.30 p.m. and 3 p.m.
Closed Sunday afternoon and Monday.

ROLLET PRADIER
8, Rue de Bourgogne, 75006
Tel.: +33 1 45.51.78.36
Just near the Palais Bourbon, the French Parliament, you will find an excellent pastry maker, one who calls himself a classic pastry chef, who goes for straightforward flavors. Among his specialties are the *blanc manger*, a bavarois dessert made with almond milk, and the Marquis, a bitter chocolate dessert. The star dessert of this pastry shop is the famous *bombe aux marrons*, a chestnut bombe comprising an almond cake layer with glacéed chestnut cream and glacéed chestnut pieces. Here it is considered a winter dessert, and this is the only season when it is available.
Closed Sunday afternoon.

STORHER
51, Rue Montorgueil, 75002
Tel.: +33 1 42.33.38.20
www.stohrer.fr
On the Rue Montorgueil, a pedestrian market street where it is fun to shop, stands a beautiful patisserie named Stohrer. The shop itself is a listed historical monument. It has kept not only its eighteenth-century decor, but also its original recipes, like the old-fashioned, high-standing *religieuse* (made only to order), the rum baba, and the *puits d'amour*. Fans of this specialty come from all over Paris for their sublime version of the cake. Vanilla lovers will not be able to resist the Chiboust tart, topped with glazed caramel. The *viennoiseries* are also of an exceptionally high standard, and the apple turnover, with its subtly vanilla-flavored apples, makes the trip worthwhile.
Open every day.
See photos pp. 1, 7, 22–23, 57

VANDERMEERSCH
278, Avenue Daumesnil, 75012
Tel.: +33 1 43.47.21.66
You'll find one of the best *galettes des rois* in this old-style bakery and pastry shop just a stone's throw away from the Bois de Vincennes. Also to be sampled are the seasonal fruit tarts, the summer *fraisier* and the Mont Blanc in fall. The kugelhopf, which is made at the weekends only, is quite outstanding.
Closed Monday and Tuesday.
See photos pp. 152, 153

Recipes for Parisian Patisseries

Those gourmands who, while reading these pages, have wished they could dive in and lend a hand, will be pleased to know that some of Paris's great pastry chefs have agreed to share their recipes with us. There are easy recipes for beginners, more sophisticated ones for established pastry chefs, and those to suit all tastes, from the most traditional to the most modern of patisseries. Here you will find tarts, *verrines*, and macaroons all within your grasp.

CAKES FROM OUR CHILDHOOD

STRAWBERRY MASCARPONE TART
Ladurée

Serves 8

INGREDIENTS
FOR THE SWEET TART CRUST
½ cup (4 ½ oz, 120 g) butter
Generous ½ cup (2 ¾ oz, 75 g) confectioners' sugar
Generous ¼ cup (0.8 oz, 25 g) ground blanched almonds or almond meal
1 pinch fleur de sel
1 pinch pure vanilla seeds (optional)
1 egg
2 ¼ cups (7 oz, 200 g) cake flour
FOR THE MASCARPONE CREAM
2 sheets gelatin
¼ cup (60 ml) whipping cream
⅔ cup (4 ½ oz, 125 g) granulated sugar
½ lb (1 ¾ cups, 500 g) mascarpone
14 oz (400 g) strawberries, washed, carefully dried, and hulled

TO PREPARE THE CRUST
Cream the butter until it is smooth. Add in the confectioners' sugar, ground almonds, fleur de sel, a pinch of vanilla if using, the egg, and, lastly, the flour. Mix only until the dough forms clumps. Gather together, wrap in plastic film, and chill for several hours. When you are ready to bake it, preheat the oven to 350°F (170°C). Remove the dough from the refrigerator and roll it out to a thickness of ¹/₁₀ inch (2 mm). It may be easier to roll it out between two sheets of plastic film or parchment paper. Sprinkle a tart dish with sugar. Carefully place the dough in the dish. Cover the dough with parchment paper and fill it with dried beans or baking beans. Bake for 20 minutes.

TO PREPARE THE MASCARPONE CREAM
Place the gelatin sheet in a bowl of very cold water until it softens. Bring the whipping cream and sugar to a boil in a small saucepan and remove from the heat. Wring the water from the gelatin sheet and dissolve it completely in the cream and sugar mixture. Set the mixture aside to cool. Whip the mascarpone until it is smooth and fold it gradually into the cooled cream. Ensure the baked crust has cooled down completely, then spread the mascarpone cream over the crust. Freeze for about 20 minutes to firm the cream. Cut the strawberries into two lengthways and arrange them attractively over the cream.
Tip: to ensure that the crust remains crisp, spread it with a thin layer of melted white chocolate (heat it to only about 86°F [30°C]), and then freeze it for 10 minutes before spooning in the mascarpone cream.

MERINGUES WITH CHANTILLY
Gérard Mulot

Yield: 6 meringues (12 shells)

INGREDIENTS
FOR THE MERINGUES
3 egg whites
1 drop natural vanilla extract
Scant ½ cup (3 oz, 90 g) granulated sugar
⅔ cup (3 oz, 90 g) confectioners' sugar, and a little extra for dusting
FOR THE CHANTILLY CREAM
1 cup (250 ml) whipping cream, 35% butterfat content minimum, well chilled so that it whips up well
2 ½ tablespoons (20 g) confectioners' sugar
1 drop natural vanilla extract

Preheat the oven to 200°F (100°C).

TO PREPARE THE MERINGUES
In a large mixing bowl, whisk the egg whites with an electric beater until they form firm peaks. Add the drop of vanilla and all the sugar in a stream, whipping continuously. Stop as soon as they are firm and glossy. Using a rubber spatula, delicately fold in the confectioners' sugar, using a circular motion. Work lightly until the mixture is just combined. Line a baking pan with parchment paper. Spoon the meringue mixture into a pastry bag fitted with a plain tip. Pipe out oval shells measuring 3–3 ½ inches (8–9 cm). Dust the shells with confectioners' sugar (a small, fine mesh sieve is useful) and wait for 5 minutes before dusting them again. Bake the meringues for 2 hours. Every 15 minutes, slightly open the oven door for 5 minutes (you may use the handle of a wooden spoon to leave the door ajar) so that the steam can escape, ensuring the meringues dry out properly. They should not change color, or only slightly. If they start to go brown, lower the temperature. When they are done, remove the baking pan from the oven and allow the meringues to cool completely before you remove them from the parchment paper.

TO PREPARE THE CHANTILLY CREAM
In a large mixing bowl, whip the well-chilled whipping cream with the sugar and vanilla using an electric hand-beater. Whip until the cream forms firm peaks. Chill until needed.

TO ASSEMBLE
Just before serving, fill a pastry bag with the chantilly cream. Pipe out a twist of cream on the flat side of half of the meringue shells. Sandwich together with another shell, flat side down. Decorate the top of the meringue with a small rosette of cream.
Serve immediately—the chantilly cream must be cold when you eat it. In summer, serve fresh berries as an accompaniment. Plain meringues will keep for over a month—in an airtight container.

MONT BLANC, SOUVENIR VERSION
Angelina

Serves 6

INGREDIENTS
FOR THE MERINGUE
3 egg whites
1 cup (200 g) granulated sugar
FOR THE VANILLA-FLAVORED CHANTILLY CREAM
½ vanilla bean
1 cup (250 ml) whipping cream
3 level tablespoons (25 g) confectioners' sugar
FOR THE CHESTNUT MOUSSE
1 leaf gelatin
1 teaspoon (5 ml) whipping cream
⅔ cup (150 ml) whipping cream
3 ½ oz (100 g) crème de marrons (chestnut cream)
3 ½ oz (100 g) chestnut paste
FOR THE CARAMELIZED CHESTNUTS
1 heaped tablespoon (15 g) sugar
1 tablespoon (15 g) butter
5 oz (150 g) vacuum-packed chestnuts, chopped
FOR THE BLACKCURRANT COULIS
3 oz (100 g) blackcurrants
2 ½ teaspoons (10 g) sugar

TO PREPARE THE MERINGUES
Preheat the oven to 200°F (100°C). Whip the egg whites. As you whip, pour in the sugar in a continuous stream. Continue until firm and glossy.
Line a baking pan with parchment paper. Spoon the beaten egg whites into a pastry bag with a small plain tip. Pipe out a spiral, starting in the centre, to make a round measuring 2 inches (5 cm) in diameter. Repeat the procedure 5 times. Then make coil shapes to serve on the side. Bake for at least 2 hours, either opening the oven door from time to time to allow the steam to escape, or with the door slightly ajar (use a teaspoon or a dishcloth) and to check that the meringue does not color too much. The meringues will keep for several weeks in an airtight container.

TO PREPARE THE CHANTILLY CREAM
Split the ½ vanilla bean lengthways and scrape out the seeds. Using an electric beater, whisk the cream with the vanilla, and then add the sugar. Continue whisking until the cream forms firm peaks. Chill.

TO PREPARE THE CHESTNUT MOUSSE

Soak the gelatin leaf in very cold water for at least 15 minutes. Wring out all the water, then dissolve it in 1 teaspoon (5 ml) whipping cream very briefly in the microwave, ensuring that it does not overheat. Whisk the ⅔ cup (150 ml) whipping cream until it forms soft peaks. Using a paddle beater, beat the chestnut cream and the chestnut paste at high speed. Incorporate the cream-gelatin mixture. Gently fold in the stiffly beaten cream until just combined.

TO PREPARE THE CARAMELIZED CHESTNUTS

Caramelize the sugar in a hot pan until it turns an amber color. Remove from the heat and add the butter. Mix thoroughly. Add the chopped chestnuts to the pan and return to the heat, stirring until they are caramelized and crisp.

TO PREPARE THE BLACKCURRANT COULIS

Process the two ingredients together until you have a coulis.

TO ASSEMBLE

Using a pastry bag, pipe out a small dome of chestnut mousse on each meringue base. Pipe out the chantilly cream over the mousse.
Place a Mont Blanc on each plate and set a meringue coil on the side. Decorate each plate with a little blackcurrant coulis. Scatter with caramelized chestnuts.
You may replace the blackcurrants with blueberries.

ELEONORE TART
Lenôtre

Serves 6

INGREDIENTS
7 oz (200 g) ready-made puff pastry
FOR THE APPLE SAUCE
1 lb (500 g) tart apples, such as Granny Smith's
¾ cup (5 ¼ oz, 150 g) granulated sugar
½ vanilla bean
Scant ½ cup (100 ml) water
FOR THE APPLE TOPPING
5 Golden Delicious apples
1 ½ cups (7 oz, 200 g) confectioners' sugar

Juice of ½ lemon (optional)
¼ cup (2 oz, 60 g) butter

TO PREPARE THE APPLE SAUCE

Peel the tart apples and cut them into quarters. Place them in a saucepan with the sugar, split vanilla bean, and water. Simmer for about 20 minutes. Chill in the refrigerator.

TO ASSEMBLE

Preheat the oven to 465°F (240°C) Roll out the puff pastry in the tart dish. Spread the compote out to just over 1 inch (3 cm) from the edge. Peel the apples, remove the seeds, and cut each of them into 8 pieces. Arrange the pieces in tightly packed rounds. Sprinkle with the lemon juice and half the confectioners' sugar (¾ cup, 100 g). Dot knobs of butter over the apples.
Bake for 15 minutes. Dust the top with the remaining confectioners' sugar to give a gloss to the fruit. Return to the oven for 5 minutes. Serve warm with well-chilled crème fraîche.

INDIVIDUAL TARTES TATIN
Blé Sucré

Yield: 4 tarts
Special equipment: 4 tart molds, diameter 2 ½ inches (6 cm), 4 dome-shaped molds, same diameter

INGREDIENTS
FOR THE SWEET BRETON CRUST
Scant ½ cup (3 ½ oz, 100 g) salted butter
Scant ½ cup (2 ¾ oz, 80 g) granulated sugar
2 egg yolks
1 ½ cup (4 ½ oz, 130 g) cake flour
2 teaspoons (8 g) baking powder
Pinch of salt
FOR THE CARAMEL APPLES
1 cup (7 oz, 200 g) granulated sugar
4 Cox's Orange Pippin, or other small-sized dessert apple
1 ½ tablespoons (20 g) butter

TO PREPARE THE SWEET BRETON CRUST

Preheat the oven to 300°F (150°C). Cream the butter and sugar together. Add the eggs, mix again, and then incorporate the flour, baking powder, and salt. Do not overwork. Roll out the dough to a thickness of less than ⅕ inch (3 mm) and line 6 small tart molds approximately 2 ½ inches

(6 cm) in diameter). Bake for 25 minutes. It is not necessary to prick or weigh down the pastry with dried beans.

TO PREPARE THE CARAMEL APPLES

Increase the oven temperature to 400°F (200°C).
Peel and core the 4 apples. Prepare a caramel with the 1 cup (200 g) granulated sugar. Pour the caramel into 4 dome-shaped molds of the same diameter as the crusts, tilting it round so that it is evenly distributed. Arrange the apples in the caramel, and place a knob of butter in the hollowed-out core. Cover with a sheet of aluminum foil. Bake for 40 minutes. When done, allow to chill for 4 hours, unmold, and arrange on the sweet pastry crusts.

TARTE TATIN
Les Deux Abeilles

Serves 8
Special equipment: a tarte Tatin pan, available in specialty shops, or a cast-iron skillet

INGREDIENTS
12 Golden Delicious apples
¾ cup (180 g) unsalted butter
Scant cup (6 ¼ oz, 180 g) granulated sugar
Approximately 10 oz (300 g) shortcrust pastry

TO PREPARE THE TART

Peel the apples and cut them into quarters.
Cut the butter into slices about ⅕ inch (5 mm) thick and line the base of the cake pan with them, placing them so that they touch the sides. Sprinkle the sugar evenly all around the pan.
Arrange the apple quarters on their sides in a tight ring around the edges. Arrange them standing in the center. Cook over a high heat for 15–20 minutes to release the juice from the apples. Then cook over medium heat until a caramel starts to form and turns from a light to a reddish color. Remove from the heat and allow to rest for 15 minutes.
Preheat the oven to 350°F (180°C). Roll out a round of pastry, about 12 inches (30 cm) in diameter, and place it over the apples, tucking the edges in.
Prick the pastry with the tip of a knife

so that the steam can escape during baking.
Bake for 15 minutes, until the crust is nice and golden.
Run a knife around the edge of the crust and turn the tart out of the pan.

CHOUX PASTRY
Lenôtre

Yield: 1 ¾ lb (800 g) choux pastry

INGREDIENTS
½ cup (125 ml) water
½ cup (125 ml) milk
Scant ½ cup (3 ¾ oz, 110 g) butter
1 teaspoon (5 g) salt
1 ¼ teaspoons (5 g) sugar
1 cup plus scant ½ cup (5 oz, 140 g) all-purpose flour
5 eggs

For the best results, choose eggs whose total volume, when cracked, is equal to the volume of liquid—1 cup (250 ml). If necessary, add another egg or half a beaten egg. Ensure that your mixing bowl is already warm when you need it.
Slowly bring the water and milk to the boil with the salt, sugar, and butter. As soon as it boils, remove from the heat and mix in the flour.
Return to the heat for 1 minute, stirring with a spatula so that the liquid evaporates.
Pour the batter into the warmed mixing bowl and incorporate 2 eggs, stirring briskly for a few seconds. Add 2 more eggs and stir briskly again. Add the last egg and stop stirring as soon as it is blended. Use the choux pastry immediately so that it does not crack.
You will probably make more dough than you will need. Pipe out cream puff shapes or éclairs and freeze them, unbaked, for up to one month.

VANILLA PASTRY CREAM
Lenôtre

Yield: 2 lb (900 g) pastry cream

INGREDIENTS
2 cups (500 ml) milk
1 ¼ teaspoons (5 g) vanilla sugar
6 egg yolks
¾ cup (5.2 oz, 150 g) granulated sugar
4 tablespoons plus ½ teaspoon (40 g) cornstarch
A knob of butter

Recipes for Parisian Patisseries

Bring the milk to the boil with the vanilla sugar.

In a mixing bowl, vigorously whip the egg yolks with the sugar until the mixture turns pale and thick. Stir in the cornstarch but do not whip any further. Pour the boiling milk over the egg yolks, whisking continuously. Return the mixture to the heat and bring back to a simmer, briskly whisking the liquid, right to the bottom of the saucepan, so that it does not stick. Allow to simmer for 1 to 2 minutes. Pour the cream into a mixing bowl to allow it to cool. Spread a little butter over the top so that it does not form a skin.

Pastry cream may be frozen, or refrigerated for 24 hours maximum. Should you need a smaller amount, you may halve the quantities: 1 cup (250 ml) milk, ¾ teaspoon vanilla sugar (2 ½ g), 3 egg yolks, ⅓ cup (75 g) sugar, 2 tablespoons plus ⅓ teaspoon (20 g) cornstarch, a knob of butter.

PROFITEROLES
Lenôtre

Serves 8

INGREDIENTS
14 oz (400 g) choux pastry (see basic recipe above)
1 ½ pints (¾ l) ice cream, such as vanilla, pistachio, or praline
FOR THE GARNISH
3 oz (100 g) chopped or slivered almonds, toasted
FOR THE SAUCE
¾ cup (2 ¾ oz, 80 g) cacao powder
¾ cup (200 ml) milk
1 scant cup (6 ⅓ oz, 180 g) granulated sugar
Scant ½ cup (100 ml) crème fraîche
2 tablespoons (30 g) unsalted butter

Butter a baking pan. Preheat the oven to 400°F (200°C).
Prepare your choux pastry and using a pastry bag with a plain tip less than ½ inch (1 cm) in diameter, pipe out about 40 cream puffs.
Bake for 20 to 25 minutes, until the pastries are golden and well puffed. Remove from the oven and allow to cool. Slit them horizontally.
While the choux pastries are cooling, prepare the sauce. Sift the cacao powder into a small mixing bowl. Combine the milk and sugar in a saucepan using a spatula, and bring

to the boil. Pour the sweetened milk over the cacao, beating constantly, and then return the mixture to the heat, continuing to beat. Add the cream and bring to the boil again. As soon as it boils, remove the saucepan from the heat and incorporate the butter.
To serve: fill the puff pastries with ice cream. Arrange them in small bowls or dessert plates. Pour over the hot sauce, scatter with toasted almonds, and serve immediately.

PARIS-BREST
Lenôtre

Serves 6

INGREDIENTS
6 oz (180 g) choux pastry (see basic recipe above)
2 oz (50 g) chopped or slivered almonds
1 egg yolk for basting
Confectioners' sugar for dusting
FOR THE FILLING
Scant ¾ cup (5 ½ oz, 160 g) butter, room temperature
2 ¾ oz (80 g) praline paste or praline powder (buy at specialty stores or online)
½ lb (250 g) pastry cream (see basic recipe above)
1 teaspoon rum or strong coffee (optional)

Preheat the oven to 465°F (240 °C). Line a baking tray with parchment paper. Trace out an 8 inch (20 cm) circle to help you pipe out the choux pastry.
Prepare the choux pastry and spoon it into a pastry bag with a round tip ⅓ inch (1 cm) in diameter. Starting at the outline of the circle, pipe out 1 circle of pastry. Pipe out a second circle just inside that, and then a third circle that overlaps the two others.
Baste the pastry with the egg yolk and sprinkle with almonds.
Bake for about 15 minutes, keeping the oven door slightly ajar with the handle of a wooden spoon. When the pastry has risen well, lower the temperature to 425°F (220°C), maintaining exactly the same opening of the oven door, and bake for another 15 minutes.
Remove from the oven and allow to cool. Cut the cake horizontally, at the base of the upper ring of pastry.

TO PREPARE THE FILLING
Soften the butter. Beat it together with the praline. Ensure that the pastry cream is well chilled and smooth, and incorporate it little by little. Whisk slowly for 2 minutes to lighten the mixture. If using rum or coffee, add it at this stage.
Spoon the Paris-Brest cream into a pastry bag with a star tip with a ¾ inch (2 cm) diameter. Fill the lower half of the cake with the cream, and decorate the rim with small peaks or rosettes.
Place the lid of the crown-shaped cake over the cream. Dust with confectioners' sugar and chill until serving.

CHERRY CLAFOUTIS
Jean-François Piège

Serves 8

INGREDIENTS
½ cup (120 g) butter
⅔ cup (120 g) sugar
2 eggs
2 tablespoons (30 ml) milk
1 ½ cups (120 g) cake flour
1 ½ teaspoons (5 g or half a packet) baking powder
¾ lb (350 g) black cherries, pitted

Preheat the oven to 350°F (180°C).

Combine the butter with the sugar. Add the eggs and the milk.
Sift the flour with the baking powder and incorporate into the batter.
Grease a clafoutis or other baking pan with butter, and then coat lightly with granulated sugar.
Pour the batter into the pan and arrange the cherries evenly over it, pushing them in lightly.
Bake for at least 15 to 20 minutes, until golden brown on top. You may want to eat it still soft, or well baked, like a traditional cake. It's up to you whether you unmold the clafoutis when it's baked. Serve warm.

Recipe previously published in *At the Crillon and at Home*, Flammarion 2008.

SALTED CARAMEL TART
Éric Kayser

Serves 8
Special equipment: one 9 inch (24 cm) square or one 10 inch (26 cm) round baking pan

INGREDIENTS
FOR THE SHORTBREAD PASTRY
½ cup (100 g) unsalted butter, softened
4 teaspoons (20 g) granulated sugar
3 tablespoons (40 g) confectioners' sugar
Pinch of salt
1 small egg
6 ½ oz (180 g) cake flour
FOR THE FILLING
1 ½ cups (300 g) whipping cream
1 ½ cups (300 g) granulated sugar
⅔ cup (150 g) salted butter

A DAY AHEAD:
In the mixing bowl of a food processor, cream the butter. Mix in the granulated sugar, the confectioners' sugar, and the salt. Add the eggs. Pour in the flour and mix thoroughly.
Form the dough into a ball, cover with plastic wrap, and refrigerate overnight.
Preheat the oven to 325°F (160°C). Line the pan with the shortbread pastry and for 25 minutes.
In a saucepan, bring the cream to a boil.
Heat the sugar in another saucepan until it turns an amber color. Gradually pour in the hot cream and butter, stirring constantly. Simmer for 5 minutes, continuing to stir.
Pour the caramel into the pastry shell and leave to cool.

Recipe previously published in *Sweet and Savory Tarts*, Flammarion, 2007.

CHOCOLATE MAGIC

FONDANT CHOCOLATE CAKES
Laurent Duchêne

Serves 6
Special equipment: 6 pastry rings, diameter about 2 ⅓ inches (6 cm), or 6 ramekin dishes.

INGREDIENTS
2 oz (50 g) bittersweet chocolate

3 tablespoons (1 ½ oz, 45 g) butter
1 whole egg plus 1 egg yolk
⅓ cup (2 oz, 60 g) granulated sugar
3 ½ tablespoons cake flour (1 ½ oz, 45 g)

Preheat the oven to 425°F (210°C). Melt the chocolate and the butter in a hot water bath. Remove from the heat as soon as the mixture is melted. Whisk the eggs and the sugar together until light and foamy.
Pour the melted chocolate and butter over the egg mixture, whisking continuously.
Pour the flour in and continue to whisk until incorporated.
Line the sides of the pastry rings with parchment paper, or butter your ramekins.
Divide the batter evenly between them. Bake for 13 minutes, or 15 minutes if using ramekin dishes. The top should be solid at the center when they are baked. Unmold the cakes from the pastry rings, or leave to cool in the ramekins.
These cakes can be served warm from the oven. If you prepare the fondant cakes ahead of time, keep them chilled, then warm them slightly in a hot oven (350°F, 180°C) or for a few seconds in the microwave (5 seconds at 600 watts).
These little cakes are delicious served with a scoop of ice cream.

BITTERSWEET CHOCOLATE TARTLETS
La Maison du Chocolat

Yield: 6 individual tarts
Special equipment: 6 individual tart molds, 4 inches (10 cm) in diameter; a cookie cutter slightly larger than the molds

INGREDIENTS
FOR THE SWEET PASTRY
½ vanilla bean
⅔ cup (5 oz, 140 g) unsalted butter at room temperature
1 tablespoon plus 1 scant teaspoon (10 g) blanched ground almonds or almond meal
2 generous pinches of table salt
Scant ½ cup (2 oz, 60 g) confectioners' sugar
1 egg
2 ¼ cups (7 oz, 200 g) cake flour
FOR THE BITTERSWEET GANACHE
7 oz (200 g) bittersweet chocolate, 60% cacao

¾ cup (200 ml) whipping cream
1 ¾ tablespoons (1 oz, 25 g) unsalted butter, in small cubes

TO PREPARE THE PASTRY CRUST
Slit the half vanilla bean lengthways and scrape the seeds into a mixing bowl. Cream the butter and vanilla seeds. Add the ground almonds, salt, and confectioners' sugar. Work lightly to combine them. When the mixture begins to form crumbs, add the egg and sifted flour. Mix until it starts to form a ball.
Place the ball of dough on a sheet of parchment paper and place another sheet over it. Roll out with a rolling pin until it is just ⅕ inch (5 mm) thick. Chill for 1 hour.
Remove from the refrigerator, peel off the top layer of parchment paper, and cut out 6 rounds big enough to fit your individual tart molds.
Place the disks in the molds, pressing down lightly so that the dough takes the shape of the mold. Trim the excess pastry from the edges (roll a rolling pin over the top for neat results).
Chill again for 2 hours.
Preheat the oven to 300°F (150°C). Prick the dough with a fork and place the tartlets in the oven for 20 to 25 minutes, until the dough is golden-brown all over.

TO PREPARE THE BITTERSWEET GANACHE
Chop the chocolate finely and set aside in a mixing bowl. Bring the whipping cream to the boil in a small saucepan. Pour it over the chocolate and leave the chocolate to melt without stirring for 2 minutes. Then, using a whisk and beginning in the center of the bowl, begin to incorporate gently with a circular movement.
When the ganache thickens, extend the circular movements outwards to obtain a smooth texture. Gradually add the cubes of butter, whisking continuously, until the ganache is silky and as shiny as a mirror. While it is still warm and liquid, divide it among the 6 tart crusts. Chill for an hour before serving.

OPÉRA
Dalloyau
Serves 12
Special equipment: square pastry mold, 10 x 10 in. (25 x 25 cm)

INGREDIENTS
FOR THE SPONGE BASE
1 ½ cups (4 ½ oz, 125 g) ground blanched almonds or fine almond meal
⅔ cup (4 ½ oz, 125 g) granulated sugar
4 eggs
1 ¾ tablespoons (1 oz, 25 g) butter
4 egg whites
1 ½ tablespoons (¾ oz, 20 g) granulated sugar
FOR THE COFFEE SYRUP
1 ⅔ cup (400 ml) water
½ cup (3 ½ oz, 100 g) granulated sugar
3 cups (700 ml) strong coffee
FOR THE COFFEE BUTTER CREAM
Scant ½ cup (3 oz, 90 g) granulated sugar
1 cup (250 ml) water
½ vanilla bean, split lengthways, seeds scraped
2 eggs, beaten
¾ cup (6 oz, 170 g) butter, softened
Scant ½ cup (100 ml) espresso coffee
FOR THE CHOCOLATE GANACHE
1 ⅔ cup (400 ml) full-cream milk
Scant ½ cup (100 ml) whipping cream
2 ¾ oz (80 g) chocolate, 70% cacao, chopped
1 ½ tablespoons (¾ oz, 20 g) butter, whipped
FOR THE CHOCOLATE GLAZE
3 ½ oz (100 g) bittersweet chocolate, 70% cacao
1 ¾ oz (50 g) cacao butter (obtainable from specialty stores and online)

TO PREPARE THE SPONGE BASE
Preheat the oven to 520°F (270°C) if your oven reaches that temperature, or 465°F (240°C) if not.
Combine the ground almonds and sugar, and add the whole eggs. Mix well. Melt the butter. Pour it in and combine well, then add the egg whites and granulated sugar. Mix until smooth.
You will need three thin layers of sponge base, so make sure the dimensions of your jelly roll baking pans are suitable. Line the baking pans with parchment paper and spread the batter out evenly. The entire surface should be covered. Bake for 10 to 15 minutes, until just lightly browned. Turn it off the pan as soon as you remove it from the oven.

TO PREPARE THE COFFEE SYRUP
Bring the 1 ⅔ cups (400 ml) water to boil with the sugar until it reaches a

syrupy consistency. Bring the strong coffee to the boil separately. Combine the two liquids and set aside to cool.

TO PREPARE THE GANACHE
Bring the milk and cream to the boil. Pour the mixture immediately over the chocolate. Add the butter and blend well.
To prepare the chocolate glaze
Melt the chocolate and combine it with the cacao butter.

TO ASSEMBLE
Cut the sponge into three equal rectangles or squares to fit into the square pastry ring you will be using. Place a layer of sponge at the bottom of the pastry ring. Moisten this layer well with the coffee syrup using a pastry brush.
Spread a layer of butter cream on this, ensuring that it is smooth. Place a second layer of sponge on the butter cream and moisten it with the coffee syrup.
Spread the chocolate ganache, making sure that it is smooth, and top with a third layer of sponge. Again moisten with coffee syrup. Top with another layer of butter cream and spread smoothly. It will be easier to spread the glaze if you chill the cake at this stage.
Finally, spread the chocolate glaze over the butter cream.
Remove the cake from the pastry square and trim any rough edges with a long, thin knife to ensure a neat finish. Chill before serving.

SOUFFLÉ
Jean-Paul Hévin

Yield: 10 individual soufflés

INGREDIENTS
FOR THE SOUFFLÉS
2 cups (500 ml) full-cream milk
1 cup plus 2 tablespoons (7 ¾ oz, 220 g) granulated sugar
2 vanilla beans, split lengthways
10 egg yolks
6 tablespoons plus 1 teaspoon (2 oz, 60 g) cornstarch or potato starch
10 egg whites
7 tablespoons (1 ¾ oz, 50 g) cacao powder
FOR THE SOUFFLÉ MOLDS
2 tablespoons (30 g) unsalted butter
2 ½ tablespoons (1 oz, 30 g) granulated sugar

Recipes for Parisian Patisseries

3 ½ tablespoons (1 oz, 30 g) confectioners' sugar

In a large saucepan, bring the milk to the boil with ¼ cup (1 ¾ oz, 50 g) of the granulated sugar and the vanilla beans. Remove from the heat and leave to steep for 5 minutes, then remove the vanilla beans. Whisk 5 of the egg yolks with a generous ½ cup (110 g) of the sugar until the mixture thickens and turns pale. Add the corn or potato starch and cacao powder and mix in well. Pour the vanilla-flavored milk over the beaten egg yolks, stirring constantly. Return the mixture to the saucepan and bring to a simmer. Allow to simmer for only 1 minute, by which time the mixture should start to thicken. Remove from the heat. Allow the cream to cool for a few minutes, then pour in the 5 remaining egg yolks, beating well. Allow to cool for 10 minutes, stirring from time to time.
Beat the 10 egg whites stiffly with the remaining sugar. Fold in ¼ of the egg whites into the cream preparation, then incorporate this mixture delicately into the remaining egg whites.
Preheat the oven to 425°F (210°C). Butter the soufflé molds and sprinkle them with sugar. Fill them to ⅔ of the height. Sprinkle with confectioners' sugar and bake for 5 minutes. Lower the temperature to 350°F (170°C) and bake for a further 20 to 30 minutes. Remove when the soufflés are well-risen, with a solid crust. Keeping an eye on the crust is a better indicator than the dry knife tip test, as by then they may be just a little over-done. Serve immediately, otherwise the soufflés will collapse.

CHOCOLATE AND COCONUT *VERRINE*
Jean-Paul Hévin

Yield: approximately 8 individual glasses
Special equipment: ramekins with a smaller diameter than the glasses in which you will serve the desserts, a candy thermometer.

INGREDIENTS
FOR THE CHOCOLATE FONDANT
7 ¾ oz (220 g) chocolate, 70% cacao mass, chopped
Scant ¾ cup (2.5 oz, 70 g) all-purpose flour
3 tablespoons (1 oz, 30 g) potato

starch (obtainable in the kosher section of your supermarket)
6 eggs
¾ cup (2 ½ oz, 70 g) sugar
2 tablespoons (10 g) shredded coconut
¼ cup (1 ¾ oz, 50 g) unsalted butter for the molds
FOR THE CREAMY CHOCOLATE GANACHE
1 ¼ cup (300 ml) whipping cream
3 ¾ oz (110 g) chocolate, with 55–70% cacao mass, chopped
FOR THE COCONUT CHANTILLY CREAM
¾ cup (200 ml) whipping cream
2 ½ tablespoons (20 g) confectioners' sugar
4 tablespoons (60 ml) full-cream coconut milk, well chilled
FOR THE GARNISH
Sifted cacao powder, toasted shredded coconut, or chocolate shavings

Melt the chocolate in a water bath until it reaches between 105 °F (40°C) and 113°F (45°C). Sift the flour and potato starch together. In another mixing bowl, whip the eggs and sugar together. Pour in the sifted flour and starch and chocolate and combine delicately until just mixed.
Preheat the oven to 350°F (170°C). Butter the ramekins and fill them with the batter. Bake for about 25 minutes. Check for doneness with the tip of a knife. If it comes out with hardly any batter on, remove the cakes from the oven and let them cool.

TO MAKE THE GANACHE
Heat the cream and let it boil for just a few seconds. Allow it to cool to 167°F (75°C), then pour it over the chopped chocolate and mix thoroughly.
Pour some of the ganache into the bottom of each glass, leaving enough for another layer. Gently unmold the chocolate cakes. Place them above the ganache and pour a little more ganache over the cake layer.
Chill for 30 minutes, until the ganache has hardened.

TO MAKE THE COCONUT CHANTILLY CREAM
Whip the cream using an electric beater until it forms soft peaks. Fold in the confectioners' sugar and the chilled coconut milk. Spoon the coconut chantilly cream into each glass. Dust with a little sifted cacao powder, toasted shredded coconut or chocolate shavings just before serving.

BROWNIES
Jean-Paul Hévin

Serves 6

INGREDIENTS
1 ¾ sticks (6 ¾ oz; 190 g) unsalted butter, softened
3 ½ oz (100 g) bittersweet (70% cacao) chocolate, melted and cooled
⅔ cup (4 ½ oz, 130 g) brown sugar
3 ¼ tablespoons (1 ½ oz, 40 g) castor sugar
3 egg yolks
½ cup (1 ½ oz, 45 g) cake flour
1 ½ tablespoons (10 g) unsweetened cacao powder
3 egg whites
1 pinch of salt
⅔ cup (2 ¾ oz; 80 g) whole or chopped pecans
A little butter to grease the baking pan

TO PREPARE THE BROWNIES
Preheat the oven to 370°F (190°C). Whisk the softened butter with the melted chocolate. Whisk in the sugars and the egg yolks.
Sift the cacao powder with the flour. Add the mixture to the batter and combine well. Add a pinch of salt to the egg whites and beat them stiffly. Add a third of the beaten egg whites to the batter and fold in. Repeat the procedure twice. Finally, fold in the pecans and combine until just mixed. Grease a rectangular or square baking pan, preferably low-sided. Pour in the batter and bake for 20 to 35 minutes. Check for doneness with the tip of a sharp knife. The brownies are done when the tip comes out practically dry. Serve warm or cooled.

CONTEMPORARY CREATIONS

ISPAHAN *MACARONS*
(ROSE, RASPBERRY AND LITCHI)
Pierre Hermé

Yield: approximately 72 macarons
Special equipment: Baking/Freezer dish, disposable gloves, candy thermometer

INGREDIENTS
FOR THE RASPBERRY JELLY
2 sheets gelatin
15 oz (420 g) raspberries
3 tablespoons (35 g) granulated sugar

FOR THE *MACARONS*
3 ½ cups 10 ½ oz, 300 g) finely ground blanched almonds or almond meal
2 ⅓ cups (10 ½ oz, 300 g) confectioners' sugar
8 egg whites (at room temperature)
4 drops red food coloring
1 scant teaspoon (4 g) approximately carmine food coloring
1 ½ cups (10 ½ oz, 300 g) granulated sugar
6 tablespoons (⅓ cup, 75 ml) mineral water
FOR THE ROSE-FLAVORED LITCHI GANACHE
14 oz (400 g) canned litchis
14 ½ oz (410 g) white Valrhona couverture chocolate or other good quality white chocolate, chopped
¼ cup (60 ml) whipping cream
3 teaspoons pure rose extract (purchase from specialty or organic stores, or online)
FOR THE COLORED SUGAR
3 ½ oz (100 g) coarse granulated sugar
A few drops of carmine food coloring

TO PREPARE THE RASPBERRY JELLY
Place the leaves of gelatin to soak in very cold water for 15 minutes. Puree the raspberries with the sugar using an immersion blender. Push through a sieve to remove the seeds. Heat ¼ of the purée to 113°F (45°C). Wring all the water out of the gelatin. Incorporate it into the hot purée. Mix well and add the remaining raspberry jelly.
Line a baking dish with plastic wrap and pour in the purée to a height of ⅛ inch (4 mm). Leave to cool at room temperature for 1 hour, then freeze for 2 hours.
Unmold from the pan and cut out ½ inch (1.5 cm) squares. Return to the freezer.

TO PREPARE THE COLORED SUGAR
Preheat the oven to 195°F (90°C). Put on your disposable gloves. Combine the sugar with a few drops of the food coloring: rub the crystals between the palms of your hands. Spread the colored sugar on a baking sheet. Put in the oven and leave to dry out for 30 minutes.

TO PREPARE THE *MACARONS*
Sift the confectioners' sugar with the ground almonds. Take 4 of the 8 egg whites and mix in the coloring. Pour this over the sugar-almond mixture without mixing.
Bring the water and sugar to a

temperature of 244°F (118°C). Prepare a syrup to make an Italian meringue. The syrup should reach a final temperature of 244°F (118°C), but before this, as soon as it reaches 239°F (115°C), begin whipping the final 4 egg whites, starting slowly and then increasing speed. When the syrup reaches 244°F (118°C), pour it in a trickle over the egg whites, whipping continuously. Whip until the temperature of the meringue cools to 122°F (50°C). Then incorporate the Italian meringue into the confectioners' sugar-almond mixture. The batter will deflate and the texture will be loose. Keep stirring to fold the mixture down a little. Scoop the mixture into a piping bag fitted with a plain ³/₈–½ inch (1–1.5 cm) tip. Line the baking pans with parchment paper and pipe out rounds of batter with a diameter of 1 ½ inches (3.5 cm), leaving just under 1 inch (2 cm) between each one. Spread out a dishcloth on the working counter and rap the pans against the counter once to remove excess air.

Sprinkle every other row of rounds with a fine dusting of colored sugar. Leave the cookies out for at least 30 minutes, until a crust forms on the surface.

Switch the oven to the convection setting and preheat to 350°F (180°C). Put the baking sheets in the oven and bake for 12 minutes, during which you should quickly open the door twice to let out steam. When they are done (when the *macaron* comes unstuck from the parchment paper), remove the sheets with the cookies still attached and leave to cool on the working counter.

TO PREPARE THE ROSE-FLAVORED LITCHI GANACHE:

Drain the litchis. Process them in a blender and then push them through a fine sieve. You should have 8 ½ oz (420 g).

Melt the chopped white chocolate in a hot water bath.

Bring the cream and puréed litchis to boil. Pour it, a third at a time, over the melted chocolate, mixing each time. Add the rose essence and mix.

Pour the ganache into a baking dish. Cover with plastic wrap so that it directly touches the ganache. Chill until it reaches a creamy consistency.

Spoon the ganache into a pastry bag fitted with the same tip as used previously.

Spoon the ganache over half the *macaron* cookies. Press a square of frozen jelly into the center, and top it with a little dollop of ganache. Cover each one with another cookie. Chill the *macarons* for 24 hours. Remove from the refrigerator just before serving.

ORANGE-BLOSSOM CREAM AND GINGER *VERRINE*
Pain de Sucre

Yield: 6 individual glasses

INGREDIENTS
FOR THE ORANGE-BLOSSOM CREAM
2 cups (500 ml) apple juice
3 sheets gelatin
4 tablespoons (60 ml) good-quality orange-blossom water
½ cup (120 ml) whipping cream
2 ½ tablespoons (1 oz, 30 g) granulated sugar
FOR THE GINGER CRUMBLE
3 ½ tablespoons (50 g) butter
¼ cup (50 g) granulated sugar
1 scant cup (3 oz, 90 g) all-purpose flour
1 teaspoon (5 g) freshly grated ginger
Zest of 1 lime

TO PREPARE THE CREAM
Divide the apple juice among the six glasses. They should be half full. Put in a straw.

Soak the gelatin sheets in very cold water until they are completely soft. Heat the orange-blossom water until it begins to simmer. Remove from the heat. Wring the water from the gelatin sheets and dissolve them in the orange-blossom water. Allow to cool a little.

Whip the cream with the sugar until it forms soft peaks. Delicately fold the slightly warm orange-blossom water into the whipped cream.

Pour this mixture delicately into the glasses over the apple juice. It will float above it. Chill for one hour, until the mousse sets.

TO PREPARE THE CRUMBLE
Preheat the oven to 325°F (160°C). Combine all the ingredients for the crumble, either by briefly pulsing in a food processor or using your hands, until the mixture forms coarse crumbs. Spread it out on a baking tray and bake for 10 minutes. Allow to cool, and then sprinkle it over the orange-blossom cream in each of the 6 glasses.

Garnish the glasses with a few pieces of fresh fruit. Raspberries are particularly attractive.

STRAWBERRY ECLAIRS
Fauchon

Yield: 10 éclairs

INGREDIENTS
18 oz (520 g) strawberries, washed, carefully dried, and hulled
FOR THE PASTRY CREAM
¼ cup (1 ¾ oz, 50 g) granulated sugar
1 egg plus 2 egg yolks
¼ cup (1 ½ oz, 40 g) cornstarch
6 leaves gelatin
1 vanilla bean
1 cup (250 ml) milk
1 knob butter
FOR THE CHOUX PASTRY
1 cup (250 ml) water
1 small pinch salt
1 pinch sugar
Scant ½ cup (100 g) unsalted butter
4 eggs
1 ½ cups (5.2 oz, 150 g) all-purpose flour
FOR THE FONDANT ICING
¾ cup (3 ½ oz, 100 g) confectioners' sugar

TO PREPARE THE PASTRY CREAM
Combine the sugar with the egg and egg yolks. Dilute the cornstarch in a little water, stirring well, and pour it into the egg mixture. Soak the gelatin leaves in very cold water until they are soft.

In the meanwhile, slit the vanilla bean lengthways. Bring half the milk to the boil with the slit vanilla bean. When it reaches boiling point, pour it over the egg mixture, beating constantly. Stir until thoroughly combined. Pour this mixture back over the remaining milk in the saucepan and simmer for 3 minutes, stirring constantly. Remove from the heat and add the knob of butter. When the gelatin leaves are soft, drain them well and dissolve them thoroughly in the cream mixture. Set aside to cool.

TO PREPARE THE STRAWBERRY CREAM
Process 14 oz (400 g) of the strawberries to obtain a juice. Stir this juice into the cooled pastry cream. Cut the remaining 4 oz (120 g) strawberries into tiny cubes, stir delicately into the pastry cream, and chill. If you are going to be piping the

strawberry cream into the éclairs rather than slitting them horizontally and spooning the mixture in, the cubes should ideally measure about ¹/₁₀ inch (3 mm) so that they don't block the tip.

TO PREPARE THE CHOUX PASTRY
Preheat the oven to 350°F (180°C). Bring the water to the boil with the salt, sugar, and butter. When the mixture begins boiling, pour in the flour and begin mixing. Allow to simmer, stirring constantly for a few minutes, then transfer to a bowl. Add an egg and stir until it is thoroughly mixed in. Repeat the procedure for the 3 other eggs. Spoon the mixture into a pastry bag with a plain ²/₃ inch (18 mm) tip, and pipe out tubes of dough about 4 inches (10 cm) long and about ¾ inch (2 cm) wide onto a baking tray. Continue the procedure leaving about 1 ½ inches (4 cm) between each éclair. Bake for 40 minutes.

TO FINISH
Spoon the strawberry cream into a pastry bag and pipe it into the éclairs, or split the éclairs horizontally and spoon in the strawberry pastry cream. For a "fondant" effect, dust with the confectioners' sugar using a fine mesh tea sieve for a fine, shiny film.

ICED CACAO *DACQUOISE* WITH CALISSON ICE CREAM AND SHARDS OF EXTRA-BITTER CHOCOLATE
Plaza Athénée

Serves 5

INGREDIENTS
FOR THE CACAO *DACQUOISE* WITH BROWN SUGAR
7 tablespoons (1 ¾ oz, 50 g) cacao powder
1 scant cup (7 oz, 200 g) brown sugar
2 cups (6 oz, 170 g) ground blanched almonds or fine almond meal
8 egg whites
¾ cup (5 ¼ oz, 150 g) granulated sugar
1 handful of chopped almond
Confectioners' sugar for dusting
FOR THE CALISSON ICE CREAM WITH EXTRA-BITTER CHOCOLATE SHARDS
½ cup (100 g) granulated sugar
¼ cup (1 oz, 30 g) skim milk powder
3 cups (750 ml) milk
11 oz (325 g) raw almond paste comprising 50 to 65% ground almonds (This means it is easily

Recipes for Parisian Patisseries

malleable. Obtainable at specialty stores and online)
5 oz (150 g) candied orange zest
4 tablespoons (60 ml) Grand Marnier liqueur
7 oz (200 g) bittersweet chocolate (70% cacao), finely chopped

Preheat the oven to 325°F (160°C). Mix the cacao powder together with the brown sugar and ground almonds. Beat the egg whites stiffly and add the granulated sugar a third at a time. When the meringue is stiff, use a rubber spatula to gently fold in the mixture of cacao, almond, and sugar. Line a baking pan with parchment paper. Spoon into a pastry bag with a plain tip and pipe out 10 balls with a diameter of 2 inches (5 cm). Scatter the lightly toasted chopped almonds over the pastry dough and dust with confectioners' sugar. Leave to rest for 2 minutes, then dust again with confectioners' sugar for a shiny effect. Bake for approximately 18 minutes. Cool on a cake rack. Keep the *dacquoises* in the freezer so that they are easier to garnish.
Prepare the calisson ice cream with extra-bitter chocolate shards
In a bowl, mix together the sugar and the skim milk powder.
Pour the milk into a saucepan and combine with the sugar and milk powder. Then bring the mixture to the boil.
Remove from the heat and add the almond paste, candied orange zest, and the Grand Marnier. Combine all the ingredients in the bowl of a food processor, using the sharp blades, or in a blender. Transfer to a mixing bowl, cover with plastic wrap, and chill overnight.
The next day, mix again and transfer it to your ice-cream maker, following the instructions.
When the ice cream is ready, serve it in scoops with the chocolate shards and garnish the *dacquoises* with scoops of ice cream.

TREATS TO GO

PISTACHIO MADELEINES
Stéphane Vandermeersch

Yield: 12–15 madeleines
Special equipment: madeleine baking pan

INGREDIENTS
Scant 2 cups (6 oz, 175 g) cake flour
1 ¼ teaspoons (4 ½ g) baking powder
3 eggs
1 scant cup (6 ¼ oz, 180 g) granulated sugar
⅔ cup (5 ¼ oz, 150 g) unsalted butter, melted and cooled
1 ¾ oz (50 g) pistachio paste (obtainable at specialty stores or online)

Preheat the oven to 425°F (220°C). Sift together 1 ⅔ cups (5 ¼ oz, 150 g) of the flour with the baking powder. Whip the eggs with the sugar for 5 minutes until foamy.
Pour in the sifted flour and baking powder, and then the cold melted butter, stirring constantly.
Add the remaining ⅓ cup (1 oz, 25 g) flour and the pistachio paste. Combine all the ingredients until just mixed.
Lightly butter the madeleine molds and fill them to ⅔ of the height with the batter.
Bake for 13 to 15 minutes, until the edges began to pull away from the sides of the molds. Keep a careful eye on the color and remove them as soon as they are done: they should retain their lovely pistachio green color.

RASPBERRY *FINANCIER* WITH SESAME OIL
Pain de Sucre

Yield: 12 *financiers*
Special equipment: baking pan with small rectangular molds, but you can also use a muffin pan.

INGREDIENTS
1 scant cup (4 ¼ oz, 120 g) confectioners' sugar
¼ cup (¾ oz, 20 g) ground almonds
6 ½ tablespoons (1 ½ oz, 40 g) all-purpose flour
Scant ½ cup (110 ml, 100 g) sesame oil, plus a little extra to grease the molds
1 heaped tablespoon (25 g) honey (lightly oil the spoon so that you can pour it easily)
3 egg whites
A handful of white sesame seeds
60 raspberries

Combine all the dry ingredients in a large mixing bowl. Pour in the oil and honey and mix using a rubber spatula. Finally, still using the spatula, pour in the egg whites and stir until just combined.
Chill the batter for 1 hour.
Preheat the oven to 200°F (100°C). Lightly grease the molds with sesame oil. Sprinkle them with sesame seeds. Fill half way with the *financier* batter. Arrange 5 raspberries in each *financier*. Sprinkle the top with sesame seeds. Bake for 10 minutes. Turn out of the molds and leave to cool on a cake rack. Best when served the same day, but these *financiers* will keep for two days.

SPARKLING LEMON COOKIES
Philippe Excoffier of the American Embassy in Paris

Serves 6

INGREDIENTS
FOR THE DOUGH
3 cups (300 g) all-purpose flour
⅓ cup (60 g) sugar
1 cup (220 g) butter at room temperature
1 pinch salt
Zest of 1 lime
Zest of 2 lemons
FOR THE "SPARKLE"
1 egg yolk
¼ cup (50 g) coarse granulated sugar

Place all the ingredients for the dough in the bowl of a food processor and pulse for 1 minute.
Divide the dough into 2 equal parts and roll each half into a log shape about 1 inch (2.5 cm) in diameter. Cover with plastic wrap and chill for 1 hour.
Preheat the oven to 350°F (180°C). Remove the dough from the wrap, beat the egg yolk and brush the logs of dough using a pastry brush. Roll them in the coarse sugar.
Using a sharp knife, cut slices about ¾ inch (1.5 cm) thick. Line a baking tray with parchment paper and bake the cookies until they are a light golden color.
Allow to cool and serve as a teatime treat.

Recipe previously published in *Elegant Entertaining: Seasonal Recipes*, Flammarion, 2009.

EDITOR'S NOTES

The pastry chefs who have contributed their recipes work with scientific precision, carefully weighing each ingredient, to achieve their spectacular results. The recipes given here are intended for you to reproduce at home, and have been converted to cups and spoons, conversions that inevitably result in some rounding up or down. Bear in mind that although this will not significantly change the end result for the more straightforward recipes, it is preferable, if possible, to weigh your ingredients.

USING GELATIN SHEETS
French chefs use gelatin in sheets or leaves, and we have opted to maintain this form for the recipes here. Each sheet weighs precisely 2 grams. Sheets of gelatin are available for purchase online or at specialty stores. To use, soak them in a bowl of very cold water (they should be completely covered) for 10 to 15 minutes. When they have completely softened, remove them from the water and wring out all the liquid with your hands. The texture will be rubbery but they will not break. Dissolve them in a little warm liquid, ensuring that there are no traces left, and then incorporate this liquid into the mixture you are preparing.

MAKING CARAMEL
Caramelizing sugar is a simple operation that nevertheless requires careful handling as caramel reaches high temperatures. Place the required quantity of sugar in a heavy-bottomed saucepan, preferably one that is light colored, and allow it to dissolve until it reaches the desired color—the darker it is, the more marked the taste will be. Do not stir, and as soon as it is done, remove it from the heat so that it does not burn. Pour quickly if that is what you need to do while it is still malleable—it will set rapidly. For less experienced cooks, it is easier to make caramel using water so you can control the cooking process better. If you use water, use proportions of 1 part water to 4 parts sugar. The end result will be the same.

Index of Pâtissiers

Index to the Recipes

Our Pâtissiers' Books

PIERRE HERMÉ
Chocolate Desserts by Pierre Hermé, with Dorie Greenspan, Little, Brown and Company
Desserts by Pierre Hermé, with Dorie Greenspan, Little, Brown and Company

CHRISTIAN CONSTANT
Everyday French Cooking, Harry N. Abrams

JEAN-PAUL HÉVIN
Délices de Chocolat, with Pierre Léonforté, Flammarion

LADURÉE
Ladurée, Instants gourmands, by Pascal Bonafoux, Flammarion

LENÔTRE
Faîtes votre pâtisserie comme Lenôtre, Flammarion
Faîtes vos glaces et votre confiser comme Lenôtre, Flammarion
The Best of Gaston Lenôtre's Desserts, Barrons Educational Series, Inc.

LA MAISON DU CHOCOLAT
La Maison du Chocolat: Timeless Classics with a Twist, by Gilles Marchal, Stewart, Tabori & Chang
La Maison du Chocolat: Transcendent Desserts by the Legendary Chocolatier, by Robert Linxe, Rizzoli

ÉRIC KAYSER
Éric Kayser's Sweet and Savory Tarts, Flammarion

Acknowledgments

The editor would like to thank all the pastry chefs who welcomed the team working on this book.
Thank you for having rearranged your displays to let us take photographs and thank you for answering
all our pressing questions about the flavors and ingredients of your creations. Thank you, of course,
for having given us the opportunity to taste so many delectable treats and thank you for your willingness
to share your recipes with us.

Thank you to Christian Sarramon who, with a great deal of talent and patience, put in long hours working
on the photography in order for every grain, every cream, every pastry, every topping, and every one
of the cakes to look their absolute best, thus giving us the pleasure of tasting with our eyes the patisseries
of yesteryear and today, and to Isabelle Ducat for her book design that showcases these delectable treats.

Thank you to Maguelonne Toussaint-Samat, whose book *La Très belle et très exquise Histoire des gâteaux
et des friandises* guided our research on the history of pastry making.

Thank you to Pierre Hermé, who kindly and enthusiastically agreed to write the preface to this book,
which aims to allow its readers to taste quality patisseries through text and image.

Thank you to Davina Koskas, Nicole Vitoux, and Robert Linxe for their valued advice, and to Safia Bendali,
Florence Faisans, Morgane Ledret, Françoise Flament, Solenn Gubri, Nadine Gavillon, Christelle Bernardé,
and Yann Brys for their gourmand's welcome.

Thank you to all those who have contributed to the realization and production of this work:
Valérie Vidal, Laurent Terrasson, Carine Ruault …

Translated from the French by Carmella Abramowitz-Moreau

Design: Isabelle Ducat

Copyediting: Penelope Isaac

Typesetting: Gravemaker+Scott

Proofreading: Helen Woodhall

Color Separation: Reproscan, Italy

Printed in Romania by Canale

Distributed in North America by Rizzoli International Publications, Inc.

Simultaneously published in French as *Délices*
© Flammarion, Paris, 2009

English-language edition
© Flammarion, Paris, 2010

09 10 11   3 2 1

ISBN: 978-2-08-030081-2
Dépôt légal: 02/2010